the
flexible
pescatarian

the *flexible* pescatarian

JO PRATT

PHOTOGRAPHY BY SUSAN BELL

WHITE LION
PUBLISHING

Contents

Introduction

'The what?' you might ask, about *The Flexible Pescatarian*. 'What's all that about?' Well, let me explain the idea behind this book and the recipes it contains, and all will become clear.

My previous book, *The Flexible Vegetarian*, was a really exciting book to write. It's aimed at anyone who eats a vegetarian diet but wants to flex the vegetarian boundaries and be given the option of adding meat or fish if they wish. The timing was perfect, as there was – and still is – an increasing trend towards eating a plant-based diet.

A totally plant-based diet is good for the environment, good for your body, good for your bank account (well, it is for mine)... but I found it quite hard work.

I figured that by providing some flexibility in the recipes it would soften the blow/sudden diet change of eliminating meat and fish altogether.

However, what I have since found is that there are a huge number of people who want to eat a vegetarian diet, but who still want to regularly include fish and shellfish and just cut out meat. This, my friends, is called a pescatarian diet (not 'a vegetarian who eats fish'!).

Everyone's reason for following a pescatarian diet will vary, but the health benefits of fish and shellfish are certainly up there. A pescatarian diet is widely accepted as being a great nutritional choice due to the excellent source of lean protein, vitamins, minerals and rich omega-3 fatty acids that various fish and shellfish provide. All of which keeps our heart, joints, skin and eyes wonderfully healthy.

For others, health isn't the main factor. It might be that they just can't commit to cutting out so many foods from their diet, but that keeping fish and shellfish satisfies their needs. For some, cutting just meat out of their diet will be for ethical and environmental reasons, and for others it will be cost.

Whatever the reason, including fish and shellfish in your diet on a regular basis is fantastic. We are spoilt for choice when it comes to varieties of fish and shellfish from all across the world – but, even though we like to eat them, many of us are scared when it comes to buying and cooking with them. Believe it or not, fish and shellfish are among the most convenient ingredients to cook – some take just minutes, making them a great choice for everyday occasions. It doesn't need to be difficult, tricky or daunting. If you follow these recipes you'll realise just how easy they are to cook.

As with all of the recipes I've written over the years, the ones in this book are carefully considered for the home cook using accessible ingredients and straightforward cooking methods. Each and every one has been tried and tested on my friends and family, and all have been given the thumbs up as ideal recipes for any occasion.

When it comes to choosing your fish and shellfish, one thing I must point out is that what you buy should be from sustainable sources. The importance of sustainability is something I cannot stress enough. Sadly, stocks of certain popular fish have been severely depleted by overfishing. So please do either ask the fishmonger or look for logos guaranteeing that the fish is from a sustainable source. There will always be alternatives or substitutions – and if your first choice of fish isn't sustainable, it's a great opportunity for you try something you may not have considered before.

If the thought of buying and preparing fish fills you with panic, then fear not: I have included lots of tips and advice in the section at the back of this book (see pages 166–176).

When you flick through the pages that follow, you'll see that many of the entries have a 'Flexible' feature at the bottom of the page. These are what

I like to think of as gold nuggets of information, offering you tips and ideas on where you can be creative with the recipe, with either fish or shellfish alternatives, or suggestions on how to make the recipe vegetarian.

You'll see that the book is structured into four chapters of delicious and practical recipes for every lifestyle and occasion.

Snacks and small plates
A variety of versatile snacks, light lunches, starters, tapas-style sharing feasts, or treats for any time of day – this chapter is oozing with flavour and fun.

Broths, soups and curries
Hearty, soul-soothing, spicy and aromatic – your tastebuds won't be disappointed by what's on offer here.

Mains and sharing
You've plenty to choose from in this fulfilling chapter, whether it's for a weekday supper, a relaxed family gathering, a smart dinner party or a BBQ with friends.

Salads and sides
Here you'll find some exciting veggie accompaniments to your main recipes, including substantial salads, vegetable dishes and hearty roast potatoes.

Whether you're new to the pescatarian diet, a longstanding and dedicated follower, or quite simply a lover of fish and shellfish, I hope you'll find plenty in this book to cook, enjoy and shout about to all your friends. I've had a great time writing these recipes and learned a huge amount. I hope you enjoy them as much as my family, friends and I do.

Jo
x

snacks and small plates

Seafood scotch eggs

*A proper picnic isn't complete
without a scotch egg, and these
prawn and smoked fish ones taste
so good, you'll want to go on a picnic
every day. This isn't the quickest
of recipes to make, but the end
result is well worth it.*

---

1 tbsp olive oil

2 banana (large) shallots, or 4 standard
  shallots, peeled and finely chopped

6 eggs, at room temperature

200g/7 oz cooked small Atlantic prawns

250g/9 oz smoked cod or haddock,
  skinned

1 tbsp chopped dill

finely grated zest of 1 lemon

pinch of cayenne pepper

¼ tsp grated nutmeg

100g/3½ oz plain flour

2 eggs, beaten

150g/5½ oz dried breadcrumbs,
  ideally panko

approx. 1 litre/1¾ pints/4 cups
  sunflower oil

flaked sea salt

Time taken 1 hour 10 minutes, plus 1 hour chilling
Serves 6

Heat the oil in a saucepan and gently sauté the shallots until they
have softened but not coloured. Tip into a food processor and leave
to cool for a few minutes.

Meanwhile, bring a pan of water to the boil then add the eggs,
ensuring they are fully covered in the boiling water. Boil the eggs
for 6 minutes, then remove and put them in a bowl of iced water to
stop them cooking further.

Add the prawns, smoked fish, dill, lemon zest, spices and a pinch of
salt to the shallots. Blend until you have a coarse paste.

Peel the eggs and roll each one in flour. Divide the seafood mixture
into six and, with floured hands, roll each portion into a ball then
flatten into a disc. Put a disc into the palm of your hand, then place
a floured egg on top of the seafood disc. Wrap the mixture around
the egg, so it is evenly covered. Repeat with the remaining eggs.

Line up the remaining flour, the beaten eggs and the breadcrumbs
in separate bowls and coat each of the seafood-coated eggs in flour,
then egg, and finish by coating in breadcrumbs. Chill in the fridge
for about 1 hour.

Fill a deep, heavy-based pan or wok three-quarters full with
sunflower oil, then heat to 180°C/350°F, or until a cube of bread
turns golden brown in 30–40 seconds. Deep-fry the eggs, two at a
time, for 5–6 minutes, until deep golden. You may need to turn them
to brown evenly. Drain on kitchen paper while you cook the rest.

Serve the scotch eggs hot or leave to cool, chill in the fridge and
serve cold.

Flexible

*To make a fish-free coating, sauté 1 chopped onion and 2 cloves of garlic in
2 tablespoons of olive oil. Blend with 400g/14 oz tinned chickpeas, drained,
½ a teaspoon of smoked paprika, 1 teaspoon of ground cumin, a small
handful of chopped coriander, and salt and pepper, until you have a
thick paste. Use this to coat the eggs before rolling in flour, beaten egg
and breadcrumbs.*

Hot smoked salmon pâté

with pickled fennel and radish salad

This dish is all prepared in advance, making it an ideal dinner party starter. Every little helps when it comes to cutting down on last-minute cooking! The crunchy pickled salad is the perfect partner for the rich, creamy pâté. I like to use hot-smoked salmon or smoked trout, as they're not too strong in flavour. However, you could quite easily switch to smoked mackerel for a more richly flavoured pâté.

For the pâté

400g/14 oz hot-smoked salmon

grated zest and juice of ½ lemon

100g/3½ oz cream cheese

100g/3½ oz Greek yoghurt

1 tbsp creamed horseradish

flaked sea salt and freshly ground
　black pepper

For the salad

200ml/7 fl oz/scant 1 cup white
　wine vinegar

50g/1¾ oz caster sugar

½ tsp coriander seeds

½ tsp fennel seeds

½ tsp black peppercorns

1 small fennel bulb, finely sliced

100g/3½ oz radishes, finely sliced

½ red onion, peeled and finely sliced

To serve

few fresh dill sprigs

grated zest of 1 lemon

toasted bread – rye or sourdough
　are particularly nice

Time taken 30 minutes, plus at least 2 hours pickling

Serves 6

To make the pickled salad, put the vinegar, caster sugar, coriander seeds, fennel seeds and peppercorns into a small saucepan. Place over a medium–high heat and stir the pickling liquor until the sugar has dissolved. Bring to a gentle simmer, and simmer for about 2 minutes. Remove from the heat and leave to cool.

Put the fennel, radish and red onion in a bowl and strain the pickling liquor over the top, removing the seeds and peppercorns. Leave the vegetables to pickle in the fridge for at least 2 hours. If you want to prepare this ahead of time, you can leave it overnight.

To make the pâté, remove the skin from the salmon and flake into a food processor. Add the lemon juice and briefly blitz. Add the cream cheese, yoghurt, horseradish and lemon zest and season with a little salt and a good twist of black pepper. Blitz until smooth.

Divide the pâté between ramekins or similar-sized dishes and smooth over the surface of each one with a palette knife. If you're not serving the pâté straight away, cover with clingfilm and keep it in the fridge.

To serve, put the pâté dishes on to plates. Garnish with a twist of pepper, a few fronds of dill and a scattering of lemon zest. Using a slotted spoon, serve some pickled salad on the side and finish by serving with toasted rye or sourdough bread.

Flexible

You can transform this into a Smoked Mushroom Pâté. Thickly slice 250g/9 oz portobello or chestnut mushrooms. Brush generously with olive oil and sprinkle or rub over 1 teaspoon of sweet smoked paprika, and sea salt. Fry for 1–2 minutes on each side, until golden. Leave to cool, then blitz with the lemon juice and continue as above. You could switch the horseradish for Dijon mustard or even onion marmalade.

Taramasalata

with tomato and olive salsa

If you've only ever had the bright pink, shop-bought taramasalata then I urge you to give this recipe a try. It's unbelievably delicious, with a subtle smoked fish flavour and rich creamy texture. Once you've made this you'll find it hard to go back!

Serve as a dip or spread on toasted pitta bread, and top with the delicious salsa. Once made, it will last up to a week in the fridge.

75g/2¾ oz dry, crustless white bread
200g/7 oz smoked cod's roe
½ small white onion, peeled
200ml/7 fl oz/scant 1 cup olive oil
3–4 tbsp lemon juice
flaked sea salt and freshly ground
  black pepper
extra virgin olive oil
pitta bread, serve

For the salsa
4 ripe tomatoes
approx. 20 black Kalamata olives, pitted
1 tbsp chopped dill or parsley
2 tsp red wine vinegar
2 tbsp extra virgin olive oil

Time taken 30 minutes, plus 30 minutes chilling
Serves 8

Put the bread in a dish and just cover in water to saturate. Squeeze out any excess water and put the bread in the bowl of a food processor.

Cut the cod's roe in half and scoop out the flesh with a spoon into the food processor. Grate the onion directly over the top, so you don't lose any onion juice. Pulse together and, with the motor running, add the olive oil and 3 tablespoons of lemon juice. Have a taste, season with salt and pepper, and add more lemon juice of needed.

Spoon into a serving dish and chill in the fridge until needed.

To make the salsa, cut the tomatoes into quarters and scoop out the seeds. Cut the flesh into small dice. Put in a bowl.

Roughly chop the olives into small pieces, and add to the tomatoes along with the dill or parsley, vinegar and olive oil. Season and gently mix together.

Heat the grill until hot. Brush the pitta with a little oil and grill until golden. Serve with the taramasalata and salsa.

Flexible
For a vegetarian alternative to serve with the salsa, give this quick smoked hummus a go. Blend 1 x 400g / 14 oz can of drained chickpeas with 1 teaspoon smoked paprika, 1 garlic clove (crushed), 2 tablespoons lemon juice and 1 tablespoon tahini. Loosen to desired consistency with a little water and season to taste with salt and pepper.

Greek bread skordalia

with charred cucumber dippers

Skordalia is hugely popular across Greece served as a dip, or as an accompaniment to fish, veg or meat dishes. There are numerous regional variations, and it can be made using either potato or bread. Here's my potato version – I like to keep the recipe really simple, with just garlic and olive oil flavouring the smooth potato dip. If you are a fan of rich mashed potato this is definitely a dip you'll love.

———————————

500g/1 lb 2oz white potatoes, peeled
  and quartered
3 cloves garlic, crushed or grated
2 tbsp white wine vinegar
1 tsp flaked sea salt, plus extra for
  sprinkling
200ml/7 fl oz/ scant 1 cup extra virgin
  olive oil, for frying
  plus extra for drizzling
6–8 mini cucumbers or 1 large cucumber,
  halved lengthways

To serve
50g/1¾ oz toasted pine nuts
½ tsp sumac, or grated zest of ½ lemon
freshly ground black pepper

Time taken 50 minutes
Serves 8

Boil the potatoes in a pan of salted water until tender, and drain well. Press through a potato ricer or, if you don't have one, mash well and push through a sieve with a rubber spatula to remove any lumps.

Transfer to a bowl and add the garlic, vinegar, salt and olive oil. Beat vigorously until you have a smooth purée. Taste and add more salt or olive oil if necessary.

Transfer to a serving bowl and set aside at room temperature.

Heat a griddle or large heavy frying pan. Brush the cut sides of the mini cucumbers with a little olive oil and place them cut-side down in the hot pan. Leave to sear for 2 minutes, until lightly charred. Remove from the heat and sprinkle with salt. If using a larger cucumber, cut into chunky wedges and griddle in the same way.

Serve the Skordalia scattered with pine nuts, a sprinkle of sumac or lemon zest, a twist of pepper and a drizzle of oil, with the charred cucumber on the side to dip in with.

Flexible
For a quicker recipe you can make Bread Skordalia. For this you need to soak 150g/5½ oz sliced white bread (crusts removed) in cold water until saturated. Squeeze out excess water and blend in a food processor with 3 cloves crushed garlic, 1 teaspoon sea salt, 1 tablespoon white wine or cider vinegar and 5 tablespoons extra virgin olive oil. Taste for seasoning, adding more if needed.

Spicy coconut prawns

These aromatic spiced prawns are really nice to serve as part of an Indian sharing platter or a starter along with the Spring Onion and Carrot Bhajis (page 39).

So I can make this recipe whenever I fancy it, I'll try and keep a bag of frozen raw prawns in the freezer. They're quick to defrost and often more economical than buying fresh. I do, however, need to lightly squeeze out excess water from the defrosted prawns in kitchen paper before marinating, otherwise they become too watery when frying.

250g/9 oz raw prawns, peeled

1 tsp ground turmeric

½ tsp flaked sea salt

¼ tsp hot chilli powder

½ tsp ground cumin

1 tsp grated ginger

1 clove garlic, crushed or grated

grated zest and juice of 1 lime

10 dried curry leaves

1 tsp dried coriander

40g/1½ oz desiccated coconut

sunflower oil

1 lime, cut into wedges, to serve

Time taken 15 minutes, plus 30 minutes marinating
Serves 4–6

Put the prawns in a bowl and mix with the turmeric, salt, chilli powder, cumin, ginger, garlic and lime juice. Marinate for about 30 minutes.

In a separate bowl, finely crumble the curry leaves into small pieces, along with the dried coriander. Add the coconut and lime zest and mix well.

Add the marinated prawns to the coconut mixture and toss to coat.

Heat enough oil in a large frying pan to cover the base and, when it's hot, add the prawns and any coconut left behind in the bowl. Fry for about 2 minutes, until golden, then turn over and continue to fry for a further 2 minutes, until golden and cooked through.

Remove from the pan with a slotted spoon and serve with lime wedges to squeeze over.

Flexible
Paneer cheese is fantastic for this recipe instead of prawns, as it holds its shape well when cooking, and it's also great at absorbing spice flavours. Cut a 250g/9 oz block into bite-sized chunks. Marinate and cook as you would the prawns in the recipe above.

Ceviche

with avocado salsa

This is a very simple ceviche recipe, where the fish is 'cooked' in a chilli and lime marinade. The end results are delicious, refreshing and super-healthy. That said – I do quite like eating this with salty tortilla chips to scoop up the ceviche, which makes it perhaps not quite as good for you!

Line–caught bream or sea bass are good here, but salmon or tuna could be used – not as delicate in flavour, but they will still give a delicious result. Whatever fish you use, make sure it is sustainable and really fresh.

---

4 very fresh sea bream, black bream or
   sea bass fillets, skinned
juice and grated zest of 3 limes
1 red chilli, deseeded and finely sliced
1 avocado, pitted, peeled and diced
2 ripe tomatoes, seeds removed and
   finely chopped
½ red onion, peeled and finely diced
small bunch of coriander, chopped
flaked sea salt and freshly ground
   black pepper
lime wedges, to serve
salted tortilla chips, to serve (optional)

Time taken 45 minutes
Serves 4

Cut the fish into 2cm/1 inch pieces and put in a bowl with the lime juice and zest, and half of the chilli. Gently mix to coat the fish in the juice, and leave in the fridge for 30 minutes for the acidity of the marinade to 'cook' the fish.

Transfer the fish to a serving plate and scatter over the avocado, tomato, onion and coriander. Pour over the marinade and season with salt and pepper.

Serve with extra lime wedges and chilli for anyone who wants more heat, along with tortilla chips to scoop up the ceviche and salsa.

Flexible
Tinned palm hearts, patted dry, sliced and marinated as above make a great vegetarian option.

Herring and potato salad

with pear marmalade

Herrings with mustard and potatoes are a Scandinavian favourite. I've taken these flavours and added a sweet 'n' sour pear marmalade, which gives you an incredibly interesting dish. This will work well for any dinner party or even as a simple lunch during the week. Once the marmalade is made it will last for a week or so in the fridge. Any leftovers are lovely with cheese and crackers.

500g/1 lb 2 oz new or salad potatoes

2 tbsp olive oil

1 tbsp white wine vinegar

1 tsp caster sugar

4 tbsp sour cream or crème fraîche

1 tbsp wholegrain mustard

1 tbsp chopped chives

8 marinated/pickled or rollmop herring
  fillets, each cut into 3 pieces

flaked sea salt and freshly ground
  black pepper

For the marmalade

50g/1¾ oz caster sugar

75ml/2½ fl oz/⅓ cup white wine vinegar

2 Conference pears

Time taken 15 minutes, plus 2 hours chilling

Serves 4

To make the marmalade, put the sugar and vinegar into a small saucepan. Stir over a gentle heat until the sugar has dissolved. Increase the heat and boil for 4 minutes.

Meanwhile, peel, core and cut the pears into approximately 5mm/¼-inch cubes. Add to the pan and simmer gently for 8 minutes, until cooked through but still holding their shape. Remove from the heat and chill in the fridge, for at least 2 hours.

Cook the potatoes in boiling salted water until tender. Drain and slice thickly, removing the skin if you prefer. While they are still hot, gently mix them with the olive oil, vinegar and sugar. Leave to cool.

When cool, mix the sour cream or crème fraîche, mustard and most of the chives in with the potatoes.

Serve the potatoes topped with the herrings. Scatter over the remaining chives and finish with the pear marmalade spooned around the outside or over the top.

Flexible

Herrings may not be everyone's choice, so goat's cheese or a salty blue cheese are good alternatives, as they both go wonderfully well with the pear marmalade and potato salad.

Chilli-baked feta

with watermelon salad

*I love the simplicity of this recipe, and
there really is nothing more delicious
than the saltiness of warm feta, spiked
with a touch of chilli and served on
top of a sweet, juicy watermelon salad.
This recipe just screams summer, and
is a fantastic dinner party starter that
can be prepared ahead of time, just
leaving the baking of the feta to the
last minute.*

½ red onion, peeled and finely sliced

1½ tbsp red wine vinegar

2 x 200g/7 oz pieces feta cheese

3 tbsp extra virgin olive oil, plus extra
   for drizzling

½ tsp dried chilli flakes

500g/1 lb 2 oz watermelon

½ cucumber

handful of pitted black Kalamata olives

small handful of mint leaves

2 tbsp runny honey

2 tsp toasted sesame seeds (see page 161)

flaked sea salt and freshly ground
   black pepper

Time taken 30 minutes

Serves 4

Preheat the oven to 200°C/400°F/gas 6.

Put the red onion in a small bowl and pour over the vinegar.
This will take out the 'bite' that raw onion can give to salads.
Set aside while you prepare everything else.

Cut each piece of the feta into four pieces. Sit a piece of foil on a
baking tray and turn up the edges to hold in any juices. Sit the feta
in the middle. Drizzle with olive oil, sprinkle over the chilli flakes
and add some black pepper. Bake in the oven for 10 minutes until
the feta has softened and is starting to get golden tinges on top.

Meanwhile, cut the watermelon into small wedges, removing any
seeds if you like, and cut the cucumber into bite-sized pieces. Put
them into a mixing bowl along with the olives, most of the mint,
the extra virgin olive oil and onions, including the vinegar. Season
with flaked sea salt and freshly ground black pepper. Spoon on
to serving dishes.

Remove the feta from the oven and transfer to the dishes. Drizzle
over some runny honey and finish with a scatter of toasted sesame
seeds and more mint leaves. Serve straight away.

Flexible

*You can switch the baked feta for grilled fish, such as tuna or
swordfish. The meaty texture is great with the refreshing, chunky
salad. Drizzle a couple of individual (approximately 200g/7oz) tuna
or swordfish steaks with some olive oil, scatter over some flaked chilli
and season with salt and pepper. Put under a hot grill for 2–3 minutes
on each side. Break into pieces and place on top of the salad. Finish
with honey and sesame seeds as in the main recipe.*

Aromatic gin and cucumber cured salmon

*Traditionally salmon was cured to
preserve it for a long time using a
combination of salt and sugar, which
'cooks' the fish by drawing out moisture
and creating a syrup. Gravadlax is
probably the most well-known version
of curing, which also includes dill and
mustard to flavour the salmon.*

*I've taken some of my favourite
ingredient combinations to give
a delicate aromatic flavour to the
salmon. It is then ready for slicing and
serving for brunch, lunch, canapés or
as an impressive centrepiece.*

---

1 side of fresh salmon, skin on and
  pin-boned
¾ cucumber, halved, seeds removed
3 tbsp juniper berries
2 tbsp coriander seeds
1 tbsp black peppercorns
100ml/3½ fl oz/scant ½ cup gin
grated zest of 1 lemon
100g/3½ oz caster sugar
100g/3½ oz coarse sea salt

Time taken 20 minutes, plus 24 hours curing
Serves 8–10

Trim any thin bits from the sides and tail end of the salmon fillet to
make it into a rough rectangle – this may seem a waste, but thinner
bits will over-cure and be inedible, so it's better to eat them now.

Grate the cucumber, and lightly squeeze out any excess liquid.
Put the cucumber into a bowl.

Crush the juniper berries, coriander seeds and peppercorns in a
pestle and mortar or by wrapping them in a tea towel and bashing
them with a rolling pin. Add to the cucumber along with the gin,
lemon zest, sugar and salt, and mix everything together.

Put two large sheets of clingfilm on to a large baking tray that is big
enough to fit the salmon. Lay the salmon skin-side down.

Spread the curing mixture all over the fish and tightly wrap in the
clingfilm. Make sure there are no holes or gaps, otherwise any liquid
will leak while the salmon is curing.

After about 24 hours, remove the clingfilm and scrape off any
of the curing mixture, then briefly rinse the salmon under cold
water and pat dry.

Using a sharp knife, thinly slice the salmon, starting at the tail end
at a low angle to remove the salmon from the skin in thin slices.

Any unused salmon will last up to 1 week in the fridge.

Tip
*Unless you know the salmon you are buying is super-fresh,
I suggest you freeze the salmon for 24 hours, then defrost in
the fridge before starting the curing process. This will kill
any parasites that could be present.*

Pea and beetroot pancakes

with cured salmon, horseradish cream and pickled cucumber

This is my fun, colourful take on smoked salmon blinis. I like to use the Aromatic Gin and Cucumber Cured Salmon (page 31) for this; however, you don't have to make your own. It will work well served any time of the year for brunch, lunch or as a sharing starter, but why not give your friends a treat by serving it as a vibrant, show-stopping canapé. The pancakes, pickled cucumber and horseradish cream can be prepared well ahead of time. All you need to do is gently warm the pancakes in the oven before topping and serving.

350g–450g/12 oz–1 lb oz aromatic
   cured salmon (page 31), gravadlax,
   smoked salmon or smoked trout

For the pancakes
75g/2¾ oz frozen peas, defrosted
75g/2¾ oz cooked beetroot
175g/6 oz self-raising flour
1 tsp baking powder
1 egg
250ml/9 fl oz milk
pinch of salt
sunflower or olive oil

For the horseradish cream
200g/7 oz crème fraîche
2 tbsp hot horseradish cream
flaked sea salt and freshly ground
   black pepper

For the pickled cucumber
½ cucumber, peeled and cut into
   1cm/½ in cubes
2 tbsp white wine vinegar
1 tbsp caster sugar
small handful of dill fronds, chopped

Time taken 1 hour
Serves 8 (makes approximately 30 mini pancakes)

To make the horseradish cream, stir together the crème fraîche and horseradish. Season with a little salt and pepper and set aside.

For the pickled cucumber, simply mix everything together and leave for about 10 minutes while you make the pancakes.

To make the pancakes, blend both the peas and beetroot separately with a hand blender until you have a smooth, vibrant green purée and a smooth, vibrant pink purée.

Whisk together the flour, baking powder, egg, milk and salt until you have a smooth batter. Divide the mixture into two bowls. Stir the pea purée into one half of the batter and the beetroot into the other.

Heat a pancake pan or non-stick frying pan over a medium heat and add about 1 tablespoon of oil. Once the oil is hot, add tablespoons of the pancake mix, giving you pancakes the size of blinis. Cook for 1–2 minutes, or until small bubbles start to appear on the surface. Carefully flip over with a palette knife and continuing to cook for a further minute or so.

Continue to make the remaining pancakes, using up both batters.

Serve the pancakes, sliced cured salmon, horseradish cream and pickled cucumber in the middle of the table for everyone to help themselves to, or assemble yourself by adding a small amount of the horseradish cream on top of the pancakes, topped with some cured salmon and finished off with a spoonful of the pickled cucumber.

Baked sardines

with capers, raisins and preserved lemon

When in season, sardines are such an inexpensive fish and so easy to cook with. Here they are simply baked with a few tasty ingredients scattered over and the end result is stunning. This dish has summer written all over it.

Serve with crusty bread for a light lunch, or with the Lemon and Bay Potatoes (p163) if you want to serve a more substantial meal.

---

8 whole sardines (approx. 85g/3 oz each), scaled and gutted
extra virgin olive oil
1–2 preserved lemons (depending on their size)
2 cloves garlic, peeled and chopped
½ tsp chilli flakes
30g/1 oz raisins
30g/1 oz pine nuts
2 tbsp capers
40g/1½ oz raisins
3 tbsp capers
small handful of chopped flat-leaf parsley
flaked sea salt and freshly ground black pepper

Time taken 25 minutes
Serves 4

Preheat the oven to 220°C/425°F/gas 7.

Put the sardines into a roasting tray or baking dish big enough for them to lie in a single layer. Pour over a generous glug of olive oil.

Cut the preserved lemon(s) into quarters, then chop the rind into small pieces. Sprinkle over the sardines along with the garlic, chilli, raisins, pine nuts, capers, parsley and some salt and pepper.

Bake in the oven for 12–15 minutes, until the sardines are turning golden. Remove from the oven and serve either hot or at room temperature.

Flexible
If sardines are out of season, then small herring or mackerel are great substitutes. For a vegetarian version of this dish, slices of aubergine cut approximately 1cm thick can be layered in the dish and cooked as above, but add on an extra 10 minutes for the aubergine to become tender.

Cornish crab pasties

I do love a Cornish pasty.
Traditionally made with a meat
and potato filling, these are given
a luxurious seafood twist. I've used
white and brown crab meat, along
with leek and potato, and an added
treat of some traditional Cornish
clotted cream as the flavoursome
filling for the buttery puff pastry
crust. They are utterly irresistible,
if I do say so myself!

200g/7 oz waxy new potatoes, peeled

1 tbsp olive or sunflower oil

25g/1 oz butter

1 leek, finely chopped

50ml/2 fl oz/¼ cup dry vermouth,
　　pastis or white wine

200g/7 oz mixture of white and brown
　　crab meat

2 tsp finely chopped tarragon or chives

finely grated zest of 1 lemon

pinch of cayenne pepper

2 tbsp Cornish clotted cream, or
　　crème fraîche

plain flour, for rolling

500g/1 lb 2 oz puff pastry

1 egg, beaten

flaked sea salt

Time taken 1 hour 5 minutes
Serves 6

Preheat the oven to 200°C/400°F/gas 6.

Cut the potatoes into small dice, about ½–1cm/¼–½ inch
in diameter. Melt the oil and butter in a saucepan over a medium
heat, and add the potato. Stir to coat in the butter and cover with
a lid. Cook for 5 minutes, stirring a couple of times, until the
potatoes are almost cooked through.

Add the leek and sauté for 2–3 minutes, until softened but not
coloured. Increase the heat, then pour in the vermouth and allow
it to almost cook away.

Stir in the crab meat, tarragon, lemon zest and cayenne, and season
with salt. Remove from the heat and finally stir in the clotted cream
or crème fraîche. Have a taste and add more salt or cayenne pepper
if necessary. It's nice to be able to taste a small amount of 'heat',
though not so much that you can't taste the crab.

Lightly flour your work surface and thinly roll out the pastry.
Cut out six circles, approximately 14cm/5½ inches in diameter,
using a plate or bowl as a guide.

Spoon the crab filling on to one half of each pastry circle, leaving
1cm/½ inch clear from the edge, Brush the edges with the beaten
egg, then fold over the pastry to seal. Crimp the edges using your
index fingers and thumbs. Place the pasties on a baking tray and
brush egg over the surface.

Bake in the oven for 25–30 minutes, until golden.

Once cooked, leave to cool for 10 minutes before eating.

Flexible
If you want to make vegetarian pasties, switch
the crab meat for diced or crumbled cheese,
such as a firm goat's cheese.

Spring onion and carrot bhajis
with green chutney

Usually bhajis are made with sliced white onion; however, these came about when I had a craving for something spicy and deep-fried. With only spring onions in the fridge I decided to give them a go. The carrot bulks the mixture out and adds a lovely sweetness and colour to the bhaji. If you want to make more traditional ones, simply switch the spring onion and carrot for three finely sliced onions and cook in the same way.

100g/3½ oz gram (chickpea) flour

2 tbsp lemon juice

½ tsp ground turmeric

1 tsp cumin seeds

¼ tsp fennel seeds

½ tsp flaked sea salt

1 green chilli, deseeded and finely chopped

2 tsp grated ginger

2 cloves garlic, peeled and crushed

bunch of spring onions, cut into long, thin strips

1 large carrot, cut into matchsticks/julienne strips

sunflower oil, for deep-frying

For the chutney

small bunch of mint leaves

small bunch of coriander, chopped

1 green chilli, deseeded and chopped

2 tsp grated ginger

½ tsp ground cumin

juice of 1 lime

flaked sea salt

Time taken 40 minutes
Serves 14–16

To make the chutney, blitz all of the ingredients together until smooth, adding 2–3 tablespoons of water, until you have a loose consistency. Taste for seasoning, and add a little more salt if needed.

Put the flour in a large mixing bowl, then stir in lemon juice and just enough cold water to bring it to the consistency of double cream. Stir in the spices, salt, chilli, ginger and garlic. Then stir in the spring onions and carrot, so they are well coated.

Fill a saucepan or wok not more than one-third full with oil and heat to 180°C/350°F. To check, a drop of batter should sizzle as it hits the oil, then float. Meanwhile, line a plate with kitchen paper.

Once the oil is up to temperature, take tablespoon-sized amounts of the mixture and carefully drop into the oil, being careful not to overcrowd the pan. Stir carefully to stop them sticking. Cook for 3–4 minutes, turning occasionally, until crisp and golden, then drain on the paper while you cook the next batch.

Serve hot or at room temperature with the chutney to dip into.

Flexible
For a twist on the recipe, swap the spring onion for 1 large white onion thinly sliced and use 1 large courgette instead of the carrot.

Grilled mackerel

with beetroot, fennel and hazelnut granola

This beautiful recipe is made up of a crunchy, sharp salad that cuts through the simply cooked oily mackerel perfectly, with the mellow, creamy addition of crème fraîche. You could just stop there, and everyone would be more than happy. However, when you serve the dish scattered with aromatic savoury granola you'll take it to another level. When stored in an airtight container the granola will keep for a couple of weeks.

---

1 red onion, peeled and finely sliced

½ medium fennel bulb, finely sliced

2 tsp caster sugar

50ml/2 fl oz/¼ cup white wine vinegar

grated zest of ½ lemon

100ml/3½ fl oz crème fraîche

4 medium cooked beetroot

4 fresh mackerel fillets, pin-boned

drizzle of olive oil

few sprigs of dill or mint, roughly chopped

flaked sea salt and freshly ground
black pepper

For the granola

100g/3½ oz jumbo oats

100g/3½ oz blanched hazelnuts,
roughly chopped

2 tbsp pumpkin or sunflower seeds

1 tbsp sesame seeds

1 tbsp fennel seeds

1 tsp paprika

1 tbsp olive oil

1 tbsp soy sauce

1 tbsp runny honey or agave syrup

1 egg white

Time taken 1 hour

Serves 4

Preheat the oven to 180°C/350°F/gas 4.

Mix together all of the dry granola ingredients. In a separate bowl mix together the olive oil, soy sauce, honey and egg white. Pour over the dry ingredients and stir well to coat in the wet mixture. Tip on to a lined baking tray and cook for 20–25 minutes, until golden brown. Stir and shake the tray halfway through, for even cooking. Leave to cool.

Put the onion, fennel, caster sugar and vinegar in a bowl and set aside to marinate while you prepare the rest of the dish.

Mix the lemon zest into the crème fraîche and season with salt and pepper.

Cut the beetroot into small wedges or chunks. Stir into the marinated onion and fennel. Season with salt and pepper.

Preheat the grill to high. Season the mackerel on both sides and drizzle with a little olive oil. Place on a baking tray skin-side up and grill for 3–4 minutes, until the skin is golden and the fish is cooked through.

Spoon some of the lemon crème fraîche on to plates, add the fennel and beetroot salad, and place the mackerel fillets on top. Scatter with the granola, a few sprigs of dill and a twist of pepper.

Tip

Enjoy any leftover granola as a snack to nibble on or to add crunch to salads, soups, roasted veggies, pasta and risotto, or even as a healthy breakfast granola with fruit, yoghurt and a drizzle of honey.

Smashed avocado and tinned sardines on toast

I've such fond childhood memories of tucking into sardines on toast at my grandparents' house on a Saturday 'tea time'. It was always the tinned variety in tomato sauce, mashed with a splash of malt vinegar and served on top of hot buttered white toast.

Now, I'll often make sardines on toast for a quick lunch when working at home. I've pimped mine up by adding a few more toppings to make them into a really satisfying meal – not to mention super-healthy.

_____

1 ripe avocado (or 2 if they are
   particularly small)
1 lime
small handful of coriander, roughly
   chopped
½ red chilli, deseeded and finely chopped
approx. 200g/7 oz tinned sardines, in
   tomato sauce or olive oil
1 tsp white or red wine vinegar
2 slices toasted sourdough, soda bread
   or crusty bread
extra virgin olive oil, for drizzling
handful of rocket or watercress leaves
flaked sea salt and freshly ground
   black pepper

Time taken 15 minutes
Serves 2

Peel the avocado, remove the stone and put the flesh into a bowl. Squeeze in the juice of ½ lime and add the coriander, chilli, a pinch of salt and some black pepper. Smash with the back of a fork and set aside.

In a separate bowl, mash the sardines and add the vinegar, a pinch of salt and a good few twists of black pepper.

Lay the toasted bread on plates and drizzle with olive oil. Spoon the smashed avocado on top, then divide the sardines between the pieces of toast.

Put the rocket or watercress leaves in a bowl and toss with a squeeze of lime, and a drizzle of oil, and season with salt. Pile these on top of the sardines and finish with a final twist of pepper.

Flexible
If tinned sardines aren't your thing, use tinned tuna. I like to mix mine with some finely diced cucumber and vinegar. Alternatively, you could pan fry some halloumi cheese and place this on the avocado-topped toasts.

Salt cod croquetas

with jalapeño and lime mayonnaise

Salt cod is cod fillet that's covered in salt to draw out moisture and preserve the fish, giving it a long shelf life. It's a popular ingredient in hot countries, and was traditionally used in the days before refrigeration. It needs to be rehydrated and de-salted before use, which takes around 24 hours. If you're looking to save some time, you could add a splash of hot chilli sauce and a squeeze of lime juice to shop-bought mayo rather than making the mayonnise below.

500g/1 lb 2 oz piece(s) salt cod
1 litre/1¾ pints/4 cups milk
½ tsp coriander seeds
¼ tsp black peppercorns
peeled strip of lemon zest
1 tbsp olive oil
3 cloves garlic, peeled and crushed
750g/1 lb 10 oz floury potatoes, peeled
    and cut into equal-sized chunks
1 tbsp chopped parsley
75g/2¾ oz plain flour
2 eggs, beaten
125g/4½ oz dried breadcrumbs,
    ideally panko
sunflower oil, for deep-frying
flaked sea salt and freshly ground
    black pepper

For the jalapeño mayo
1 jalapeño chilli
½ tsp salt
1 egg yolk
½ tsp Dijon mustard
1 tbsp lime juice
250ml/9 fl oz/1 cup sunflower oil

Time taken 1 hour 15 minutes, plus 24 hours soaking beforehand, and 1 hour chilling
Makes 16–18 croquetas

First you need to soak the cod. You'll need to start this process a full day before making the croquetas to remove the salt and rehydrate the fish. Put the cod in a large bowl and cover with plenty of cold water. Leave at room temperature for 24 hours, changing the water at least four times.

Put the cod into a frying pan and pour over half of the milk. Add the coriander seeds, peppercorns and lemon zest. Bring to a gentle simmer and heat for 10 minutes, loosely covering the pan with a lid. Drain the fish and flake it into a bowl, removing any skin and bones.

Meanwhile, put the olive oil and garlic in a medium–large non-stick saucepan and place over a medium heat. Once the oil is hot and the garlic starts to sizzle but not colour, add the potatoes and the remaining milk to completely cover the potatoes (adding a little more milk if needed).

Add a pinch of salt, bring the potatoes to a simmer, cover loosely with a lid and cook over a low heat for about 15 minutes, until the potatoes are tender. Drain off the milk and mash the potatoes until really smooth. Add the flaked cod, chopped parsley and a twist of black pepper. Mix well to combine and season with pepper and salt to taste (you may not need any salt, depending on how salty the cod is).

Shape the mixture into 16–18 cylinder shapes using your hands. Keep a bowl of cold water to the side to wet your hands and prevent the mixture sticking.

Put the flour, eggs and breadcrumbs into three separate bowls. Lightly coat each croqueta in flour, then dip in egg and finish by evenly coating in breadcrumbs. Chill in the fridge for about 1 hour, or until needed.

To make the mayonnaise you need to roast the jalapeño all over
to blister the skin and soften the flesh. This can either be done by
holding it over a gas flame (using a pair of tongs) or putting it under
a hot grill, turning a couple of times. Once charred and soft, set
aside to cool for a few minutes.

Roughly chop the jalapeño, removing the stalk, and put it into a
small food processor or hand blender jug along with the salt. Blend
to roughly chop. Add the egg yolk, mustard and lime juice and, with
the motor running, slowly pour in the oil, to emulsify, thicken and
create a mayonnaise. If it starts to split, add a little water and blend
again. Taste for seasoning, adding more salt or lime juice if needed.
Set aside or keep covered in the fridge for up to 2 days.

To cook the croquetas, heat the oil in a wide, deep heavy-based pan,
no more than half-full, to 190°C/375°F (use a thermometer, or drop
in a piece of bread; it should turn golden in about 35 seconds), or
use a deep-fat fryer. Lower half of the croquetas into the hot oil, and
cook for about 2–3 minutes, until golden and crisp.

Remove from the hot oil with a slotted spoon and drain on kitchen
paper. Repeat with the remaining croquetas. Serve hot with the
jalapeño mayonnaise.

Flexible
*You'll end up with a very different flavour and textured filling,
but if you like the sound of this recipe and need a quicker
version, you can use tinned tuna rather than salt cod. Ideally
use tuna in water rather than oil and drain it well, giving you a
total of 500g / 1 lb 2oz of fish. Mix with the cooked mash, parsley
and pepper. A good pinch of salt will also be needed, and some
grated lemon zest too. Shape into croquetas and cook as above.*

Clams

with sherry, garlic and tomatoes

It's hard to believe you can create so much flavour in such a short space of time with this tapas-style dish. The sweet, juicy clams cooked in rich tomato, dry sherry and fragrant garlic with a hint of hot, smoky paprika in the background is unbelievably delicious. Serve with chilled fino sherry, and you've a match made in Spanish heaven.

---

4 tbsp olive oil

4 cloves garlic, crushed

1 tsp hot smoked paprika

pinch of saffron

150ml/5 fl oz/⅔ cup dry sherry

400g/14 oz tin chopped tomatoes

2 tsp sherry vinegar

1kg/2 lb 4 oz fresh clams

small bunch of flat-leaf parsley, chopped

flaked sea salt and freshly ground
   black pepper

crusty bread, to serve

Time taken 20 minutes

Serves 4

Heat a frying pan over a medium heat. Add the olive oil, garlic, smoked paprika and saffron. Gently cook for about 1 minute, stirring all the time so the garlic doesn't burn.

Pour in the sherry, tomatoes and vinegar and season with salt and pepper. Increase the heat and allow to simmer for 5 minutes.

Meanwhile, wash the clams in cold water, discarding any that don't show signs of closing when lightly squeezed.

Stir the clams into the tomato and sherry sauce. Cover with a lid and cook, giving the pan a shake every so often, for 2–3 minutes, until the all the clams have opened. Discard any clams that refuse to open at all.

Stir in the parsley, taste for seasoning, and serve with some crusty bread.

Flexible

Try replacing the clams with the same weight of mussels, or you could also use 400g / 14 oz sliced squid, raw prawns or even white beans, such as cannellini or butter beans. Add to the sauce at the same time as the chopped tomatoes and leave to cook for 5 minutes.

Smoky Padrón peppers

The key to getting the best out of these is to serve them hot and keep your fingers crossed you don't get a really spicy one. Usually about one in ten is fiery – eating them is a bit like a game of Russian roulette! To pimp these up a bit I like to add some smoked paprika with the sea salt at the end. Use hot paprika if you fancy additional heat, especially if you think they won't be spicy at all.

---

olive oil

150g/5½ oz Padrón peppers

½ tsp smoked paprika (hot or sweet)

flaked sea salt

Time taken 5 minutes

Serves 4

Place a large heavy frying pan (cast iron if you have one) over a medium–high heat. Add enough oil to cover the surface of the pan. Once the oil starts to shimmer, just before it starts to smoke, put the peppers in the pan in a single layer. Don't overcrowd the pan as they won't cook properly. Cook the peppers in a couple of batches if need be.

Cook the peppers for 2 minutes, turning now and then, until the skins are golden and blistered and the flesh is softened.

Sprinkle with the paprika and a good pinch of sea salt.

Remove the peppers with a slotted spoon and put them on some kitchen paper to absorb any excess oil. Transfer them to a serving dish and sprinkle with a little more salt. Serve straight away.

Flexible

Though this is traditionally made using Padrón peppers, I gave the same idea a try using okra – and to my surprise, it was delicious! Make sure you cook it on a high heat so it stays slightly crunchy in the middle and becomes golden on the outside. Obviously you don't have the occasional hot one when it comes to okra, so if it's a bit of heat you like, then opt for the hot smoked paprika when cooking it.

Slow-roasted sweet potato

with feta, pomegranate and pistachios

Sometimes just combining a few simple ingredients gives the most satisfying results. There's something to tick every box in this recipe: sweet, melt-in-the mouth potato, salty cheese, tangy pomegranate molasses, crunchy pistachios and juicy pomegranate seeds – oh, and not to mention the slightly smoky, crunchy potato skin that really should not be left behind on the plate. Every time I look at this picture I just want to eat it there and then.

---

2 medium sweet potatoes, scrubbed

1 tbsp sunflower oil

½ tsp smoked or sweet paprika

1 tsp flaked sea salt

50g/1¾ oz pistachios

2 tbsp pomegranate seeds

4 spring onions, finely sliced

100g/3½ oz feta cheese, crumbled

extra virgin olive oil

1 tbsp pomegranate molasses

few mint leaves

Time taken 1 hour

Serves 2

Preheat the oven to 200°C/400°F/gas 6.

Prick the sweet potatoes all over with a fork. Put into a bowl along with the oil, paprika and salt. Rub or toss to coat the potatoes in the spicy oil. Put the potatoes in the oven and bake for 45–55 minutes, or until tender and the skin is crisp.

To serve, cut open the sweet potatoes and scatter each half with the pistachios, pomegranate seeds, spring onions and crumbled feta. Drizzle with extra virgin olive oil and some pomegranate molasses.

Finish with some mint and enjoy while the potatoes are still hot.

Flexible

Smoked mackerel or hot smoked salmon are both really good alternatives to the feta cheese. Break into flakes and serve as above.

Smoked hash

with chilli eggs

*Brunch, lunch, late-night supper
… I could eat this any time. Crispy
potatoes, caramelised onions, smoky
flakes of fish and topped with a fried
egg and drizzled with chilli sauce.
What's not to love?*

750g/1 lb10 oz Charlotte or
   salad potatoes
olive oil
1 large red onion, peeled and sliced
½ tsp smoked paprika
250g/9 oz smoked mackerel, hot-smoked
   salmon or smoked trout
4 eggs
handful of chopped flat-leaf parsley
chilli or peri-peri sauce
flaked sea salt and freshly ground
   black pepper

Time taken 40 minutes
Serves 4

Cook the potatoes in boiling salted water for about 15 minutes, until
they are just tender. Drain, and, when cool enough to handle, cut in
half or quarters depending on their size.

Heat a large, non-stick frying pan with enough olive oil to cover the
surface. Add the onion, and cook over a medium heat until softened.
Add the potatoes and smoked paprika, increase the heat and fry
until both the potatoes and onion are golden and becoming crunchy.

Flake in the smoked mackerel, salmon or trout and toss to heat
through. Season with salt and pepper and scatter with the parsley.

In a separate pan, heat approximately 1 tablespoon of olive oil and
break in the eggs, frying until they start turning crisp around the
edges but the yolk is still runny.

Spoon the smoked hash on to plates, top with the fried eggs and
drizzle with chilli or peri-peri sauce.

Flexible
*Smoked fish can be replaced with 400g/14 oz tinned
cannellini, kidney, butter or black-eyed beans. Drain
well and add to the crunchy potatoes, frying for a
couple of minutes. As you are missing the smoky
flavour from the fish, you can increase the amount of
smoked paprika to 1 teaspoon.*

Fish fingers

and a handful of dips

Impossible to resist, homemade fish fingers are the best. You can use most types of fish – the chunkier the fish, the bigger your fingers. If you want daintier goujons, opt for a flat fish such as sole, plaice or dab.

Serve with one or all of the five dips, which are all easy to prepare and delicious with fish fingers, fried fish or pretty much any fish dish.

450g/1 lb white fish, skinned
50g/1¾ oz plain flour
2 eggs, beaten
100g/4½ oz dried white breadcrumbs,
  ideally panko
1 tsp paprika
1 tsp flaked sea salt
olive oil, for frying
freshly ground black pepper

Time taken 30 minutes
Serves 4

Cut the fish into finger-sized pieces.

Put the flour, beaten egg and breadcrumbs into separate shallow bowls. Mix the paprika, salt and a twist of pepper into the flour. Lightly coat the fish in the flour, then egg, and finish with a coating of breadcrumbs.

To fry the fish fingers, pour in enough oil to cover the base of a frying pan and, when it's hot, add the fish fingers. Fry for 2–3 minutes on each side until golden and crunchy. You may need to do this in a couple of batches, as it's best not to overcrowd the pan. Drain on kitchen paper and serve with your chosen dips.

Alternatively, you can bake the fish fingers by putting them on an oiled baking tray and drizzling or spraying with oil. Bake in a preheated oven at 200°C/400°F/gas 6 for 6 minutes on each side.

Olive oil hollandaise dip

175ml/6 fl oz olive oil
finely grated zest of ½ lemon
2 egg yolks
2 tbsp lemon juice
2 tbsp water
pinch of cayenne pepper
flaked sea salt

Time taken 10 minutes
Serves 4

Warm the olive oil and lemon zest in a small pan until just tepid.

Place the egg yolks, lemon juice and water in a medium heatproof bowl. Stand the bowl in a pan of gently simmering water and whisk until the mixture thickens just enough to form ribbons when the whisk is lifted.

Remove the bowl from the pan and slowly pour the warm oil into the egg mixture, whisking continuously to give you a dipping sauce consistency. Season with salt and a pinch of cayenne pepper. Keep covered until needed.

Cocktail dip

Time taken 5 minutes
Serves 4

100ml/3½ fl oz mayonnaise
4 tbsp tomato ketchup
juice of ½ lemon
1 tbsp Worcestershire sauce
few drops of Tabasco sauce
½ tsp paprika
flaked sea salt and freshly ground black pepper

Mix everything together and transfer
to a serving dish.

Pea and mint

Time taken 10 minutes
Serves 4

150g/5½ oz frozen peas, defrosted
4 tbsp crème fraîche
small handful of mint leaves
grated zest of 1 lemon
1 tbsp lemon juice
1 tbsp extra virgin olive oil
flaked sea salt and freshly ground black pepper

Put the peas in a food processor and
briefly blitz before adding the remaining
ingredients. Blend until smooth and transfer
to a serving bowl.

Wasabi and lime mayo

Time taken 5 minutes
Serves 4

125ml/4 fl oz mayonnaise
1 tbsp wasabi
2 tsp lime juice

Mix the wasabi and lime into the mayonnaise
and transfer to a serving bowl.

Tartare

Time taken 10 minutes
Serves 4

150ml/5½ fl oz mayonnaise
2 tbsp capers
3 tbsp finely chopped gherkins
½ shallot, peeled and finely chopped
squeeze of lemon juice
2 tbsp chopped flat-leaf parsley
flaked sea salt and freshly ground black pepper

Mix everything together and transfer
to a serving bowl.

broths, soups
and curries

Chilled pea and tarragon soup

with brown shrimp and goat's curd toasts

This soup is great on its own, and even better with the toasts. Both are quick and simple to make with flavours that go so well with the fragrant pea soup. Should you struggle getting hold of brown shrimps, you can use small prawns. Goat's curd is very soft and delicate in flavour, and is becoming far more available – but again, if you can't get any, don't worry, as a mild creamy goat's cheese will be just fine for these toasts.

———————————————

2 tbsp olive oil

1 onion, peeled and finely chopped

1 stick of celery, finely chopped

500g/1 lb 2 oz frozen peas

5g tarragon leaves, plus some sprigs
  to serve

600ml/20 fl oz/2½ cups hot vegetable stock

½ tsp caster sugar

75g/2¾ oz crème fraîche

few pea shoots

flaked sea salt and freshly ground
  black pepper

extra virgin olive oil, for drizzling

For the brown shrimp toasts

4–6 small rounds baguette or similar

80g/3 oz brown shrimps

25g/1 oz melted butter

finely grated zest of ¼ lemon

pinch of cayenne pepper

pinch of grated nutmeg

For the goat's curd toasts

4–6 small rounds baguette or similar

100g/3½ oz goat's curd or soft
  goat's cheese

finely grated zest of ¼ lemon

½–1 tsp capers

Time taken 40 minutes

Serves 4–6

Heat the oil in a medium–large saucepan. Add the onion and celery. Gently sauté for about 8 minutes, until soft but not coloured. Stir in the peas, tarragon, stock and sugar. Increase the heat, bring to the boil and cook for 3 minutes.

Meanwhile fill a large bowl with ice and cold water. Place another bowl on top of the ice.

Remove the soup from the heat and stir in the crème fraîche. Quickly blend the soup until smooth, preferably with a stick blender for ease and speed. Pass through a sieve into the bowl inside the iced water bowl (this will quickly chill the soup, keeping it a vibrant green colour).

Season, and stir until cool. Cover and chill in the fridge until needed.

Toast all of the bread until lightly golden.

Mix together the shrimps, melted butter, lemon zest, cayenne pepper and nutmeg. Taste for seasoning, and add some salt if necessary. Spoon on top of half of the toasts and finish with a pinch of cayenne pepper on top of each one.

Top the remaining toasts with some goat's curd. Scatter over some lemon zest, a few capers and a twist of black pepper.

Spoon the chilled soup into bowls and garnish with a twist of pepper, a few pea shoots and a drizzle of extra virgin olive oil. Serve the toasts on the side.

Flexible
Pea and mint is an equally tasty combination, so feel free to swap tarragon for mint in the soup.

Steamed mussels

with creamy cider broth

This is my fruity twist on the incredible French dish of moules marinières. Instead of white wine I've used cider, which works so well with the sweet juicy mussels, and the diced Bramley apple adds a sharpness to the creamy sauce. This really can't be eaten elegantly, so embrace it and use your fingers to pick up the mussel shells, and have plenty of fresh crusty bread on hand to mop up the juices.

---

1 kg/2 lb 4 oz fresh mussels
1 tbsp olive oil
50g/1¾ oz butter
1 leek, finely chopped
2 cloves garlic, peeled and crushed
1 medium Bramley apple, peeled
  and diced
400ml/14 fl oz/1 ⅔ cups sweet cider
200ml/7 fl oz/scant 1 cup single cream
2 tsp Dijon mustard
small bunch of flat-leaf parsley, chopped
flaked sea salt and freshly ground
  black pepper
crusty bread, to serve

Time taken 30 minutes
Serves 4

Wash the mussels and pull off any 'beards' that are attached at the end of the shell. Discard any mussels that are open and don't close when lightly pinched together, and any with damaged shells.

Place a large saucepan over a medium heat. Add the olive oil and butter. When the butter has melted and starts to bubble, add the leek, garlic and apple. Sauté until the leeks are tender and the apple has started to break down to a pulp.

Increase the heat and add the cider, cream and mustard, and season with salt and pepper. Bring to the boil, then throw in the mussels. Stir around, then cover the pan with a tight-fitting lid. Cook for 3 minutes, shaking the pan a couple of times, then check to see if the mussels have opened. If not, replace the lid and continue to cook for a further 1 minute, or until the mussels are all open.

Scatter over the parsley and divide between bowls. Discard any mussels that have refused to open.

Serve hot, with crusty bread to mop up the creamy cider broth.

Flexible
Mussels aren't available all year round. If you can't get hold of any but see some clams, then grab a net of those instead. They are smaller but just as tasty, and work well with this sauce.

Roast vegetable vindaloo

with pickled red onion rings

Despite the long list of ingredients, this is a really straightforward recipe. The powerful vindaloo spice paste can be made ahead of time and kept in the fridge ready to roast with the vegetables whenever you need it. Be prepared: this is a pretty hot and spicy paste, but the tangy pickled onion rings really cut through the spice and your mouth is left feeling alive … not on fire!

1.5kg/3 lb 5 oz root vegetables, such as
    carrot, beetroot, sweet potato, squash,
    celeriac, parsnip, potato
2 onions, peeled and cut into wedges
3 tsp chilli flakes
2 tsp whole cloves
2 tsp coriander seeds
1 tsp cumin seeds
1 tsp ground turmeric
2 tsp flaked sea salt
seeds from 10 cardamom pods
1 tbsp lemon juice
5 tbsp sunflower oil
4 cloves garlic, peeled and chopped
25g/1 oz ginger, peeled and chopped
2 tbsp gram (chickpea) flour
1 tbsp tomato purée
350ml/12 fl oz/1½ cups hot
    vegetable stock

For the pickled red onions
150ml/5 fl oz/⅔ cup cider or white wine
    vinegar
2 tbsp sugar
1 star anise
1 cinnamon stick, broken in half
2 red onions, peeled and sliced into rings

Time taken 1 hour 30 minutes, plus overnight pickling
Serves 4

To make the pickled red onions, gently heat the vinegar in a small saucepan with the sugar, star anise and cinnamon. Stir until the sugar has dissolved. Pour over the onions and leave for at least 2 hours, but overnight is better.

Preheat the oven to 200°C/400°F/gas 6.

Cut the root vegetables into similar-sized pieces to the wedges of onion. Put them all into a large, deep roasting tray, or two if you're struggling to fit them all in one.

Blend together the chilli flakes, cloves, coriander seeds, cumin seeds, turmeric, salt, cardamom pods, lemon juice, sunflower oil, garlic and ginger in either in a small blender or by hand using a pestle and mortar, until combined.

Spoon the spice paste on to the vegetables and mix until they are coated. Roast for about 30–40 minutes, turning occasionally, until the vegetables are tender and golden.

Remove the tray from the oven. Scatter over the gram flour and gently turn the vegetables to coat them in the flour.

Mix the tomato purée into the hot stock and pour over the vegetables. Return the roasting tray to the oven, and continue to cook for 10 minutes, until you have a thick sauce just coating the vegetables.

Serve the spicy roasted vegetables with rings of the pickled onions, drained from their pickling liquor, and a green vegetable of your choice.

Flexible
For a seafood twist, toss in some peeled raw prawns for the final 10 minutes of cooking time.

Quick Moroccan tomato and bread soup

If you've a few ripe tomatoes to use up and some bread past its best, this is what you should make. It's a simple soup that's been given a huge boost of Middle Eastern flavour from basic store-cupboard spices. Any soup that's not eaten straight away will thicken up, so just add a splash of water or stock when reheating. I'll often make this and freeze it in portions so I've got an instant lunch on days when I'm working at home.

---

2 tbsp olive oil

1 onion, peeled and finely chopped

1 tsp paprika

¼ tsp ground cinnamon

¼ tsp ground cumin

½ tsp ground ginger

75g/2¾ oz chunk of bread, preferably
  quite dry and past its best

450–500g/1–1 lb 2 oz very ripe tomatoes,
  roughly chopped

1 tsp harissa

small handful of fresh coriander

flaked sea salt and freshly ground
  black pepper

To serve (optional)

3–4 tbsp labneh, Greek yoghurt,
  or crumbled feta cheese

1 preserved lemon, chopped

fresh coriander leaves

small handful of chopped pistachios
  or flaked almonds

1 tsp harissa

Time taken 30 minutes
Serves 4

Heat the olive oil in a saucepan and add the onion, paprika, cinnamon, cumin and ginger. Cook gently for about 5–6 minutes, until the onion is nicely softened.

Tear the bread into small pieces and add it to the pan along with the tomatoes, harissa and 150ml/5 fl oz/⅔ cup water. Cook for 10–12 minutes over a medium heat, until the tomatoes have softened and are starting to break down.

Transfer to a blender with the coriander and blitz until smooth, or use a stick blender. Season with salt and pepper. If the soup seems too thick, add a splash of water to loosen it.

Reheat as needed and spoon into bowls. Serve the soup as it is, or with a dollop of labneh or Greek yoghurt or crumbled feta cheese on top, and a scattering of preserved lemon, coriander leaves, pistachios and a drizzle of harissa for added spice.

Flexible
For a seafood finish, add cooked prawns or marinated anchovies on top of the soup when serving.

Smoky haddock and clam chowder

This is a really hearty chowder that's packed with flavour. Steaming the clams in white wine creates a fantastic 'stock', which is used to make the creamy broth for cooking the smoked haddock, locking in every possible bit of flavour. Even though it's quick enough for a midweek meal, it is also elegant enough to serve as a dinner party dish.

500g/1 lb 2 oz fresh clams
250ml/9 fl oz/1 cup white wine
2 tbsp olive oil
2 banana shallots or 4 standard shallots, finely chopped
1 bay leaf
¼ tsp ground allspice
pinch of cayenne pepper
20g/¾ oz plain flour
2 medium baking potatoes, peeled and diced into 2cm/¾ in cubes
400ml/14 fl oz/1½ cups milk
500g/1 lb 2 oz smoked haddock, skinned
150ml/5 fl oz/⅔ cup single cream
1 tbsp chopped parsley
1 tbsp chopped chives
flaked sea salt and freshly ground black pepper

Time taken 40 minutes
Serves 4

Wash the clams in cold water, discarding any that don't show signs of closing when lightly squeezed.

Heat a large saucepan with a tight fitting lid over a high heat. When hot, add the wine and clams. Immediately cover with the lid and steam for 3 minutes until the clam shells open. Drain in a colander set over a bowl to catch the juices, and discard any clams that won't open.

Heat the oil in a large saucepan and add the shallots, bay leaf, allspice and cayenne pepper. Gently sauté for about 8 minutes, until the shallots are nicely softened and starting to become golden.

Stir in the flour and cook for about 30 seconds before adding the potatoes, clam juices and milk, stirring so the flour doesn't form lumps. Bring to a simmer and cover loosely with a lid. Cook for 8 minutes, or until the potatoes are almost cooked through.

Cut the smoked haddock into bite-sized pieces and add to the pan. Loosely cover with the lid again and gently simmer for 4 minutes, until the fish is just cooked.

Stir through the clams, cream, parsley and chives, and season with salt and pepper. Add a splash more milk if the chowder is too thick, and serve hot.

Flexible
You can make this into a smoked haddock chowder by replacing the clams with an additional 250g/9 oz smoked haddock. Instead of using white wine, the same quantity of fish stock can be used.

Malaysian prawn and pineapple curry

*There are times when I am all for
using a bought curry or spice paste,
but for this recipe you just can't
cut corners. It's not difficult or
time-consuming, and the end result
is well worth it. This is such a
colourful curry, which is mild in spice
yet packed with aromatic flavour
and juicy textures coming from the
pineapple and prawns.*

---

sunflower oil

4 tbsp desiccated coconut

3 cloves garlic, peeled and grated
or crushed

1 tbsp ginger, grated

1 tbsp mild or medium curry powder

½ tsp turmeric

1 cinnamon stick

½ tsp cardamom pods, lightly crushed

½ tsp whole cloves

1 star anise

3 banana (large) shallots or 6 regular
shallots, sliced

1 medium ripe pineapple, peeled,
cored and cut into chunks (about
350g/12 oz when prepped)

400ml/14 fl oz tin coconut milk

1 tbsp light brown sugar

1 tbsp fish sauce

400g/14 oz large raw prawns, peeled

handful of coriander leaves

cooked basmati or jasmine rice, to serve

Time taken 45 minutes
Serves 4

Heat 2 tablespoons of oil in a wok or large saucepan and add the
desiccated coconut. Cook until it's deep golden. Transfer to a bowl
and mix in the garlic, ginger, curry powder, turmeric, 1 teaspoon
of salt and 2 tablespoons of water to make a paste.

Return the wok to the heat and add 3 tablespoons of oil. When it's
shimmering, add the cinnamon, cardamom, cloves and star anise.
Cook for about 30 seconds until they become aromatic, then add
the shallots. Reduce the heat and stir the shallots around in the
pan until they are golden.

Add the coconut paste and cook over a low heat, stirring
occasionally to prevent it from sticking too much to the bottom
of the pan, for about 2 minutes.

Add the pineapple, coconut milk, sugar and fish sauce. When the
coconut milk has come to a simmer, stir in the prawns. Cook for
a few minutes until the prawns have turned pink. Taste for
seasoning and either add some more fish sauce or some salt.

Stir through the coriander and serve the curry with rice.

Flexible
*To transform this into a vegetarian curry, diced
butternut squash is great. It needs a longer
cooking time than prawns, so I recommend cutting
it pretty small (about the size of the prawns),
adding it with the coconut milk and cooking for
8 minutes before stirring in the pineapple and
cooking for a further 2 minutes.*

Smoky bean and monkfish stew

This stew is simple and quick to cook, and has a Spanish feel to it. Monkfish is a fantastic fish, as it holds itself really well in stews and curries, and is also able to stand up to bold flavours. It's not necessarily the cheapest of fish, so if you want to use an alternative, prawns, cod cheeks, hake or gurnard will all work really well in this dish.

500g/1 lb 2 oz monkfish fillet

2 tbsp olive oil

2 onions, peeled and sliced

4 cloves garlic, peeled and chopped

1½ tsp smoked paprika

1 tbsp tomato purée

400g/14 oz tinned cannellini, butter or
   haricot beans, drained

1 roasted red pepper, thinly sliced

850ml/1½ pints/3½ cups fish stock

1 bay leaf

handful of chopped flat-leaf parsley

flaked sea salt and freshly ground
   black pepper

Time taken 40 minutes

Serves 4

Cut the monkfish into equal-sized pieces and season with salt and pepper. Set aside.

Heat a large pan over a medium heat and add the olive oil. When hot, add the onions and gently sauté for 5–6 minutes, until they are softened and starting to colour. Stir in the garlic, paprika and tomato purée, and continue to cook for a further 1–2 minutes.

Add the beans, red pepper, stock and bay leaf. Bring to a simmer and cook uncovered for 15 minutes.

Stir the monkfish into the stew, return to a simmer and cook gently for 5 minutes. Stir in the parsley, and season to taste.

Divide between bowls and serve hot.

Flexible
The end result will be pretty different, but to make this a vegetarian stew, you can swap the monkfish for double the amount of beans. I like to use a mixture of beans to create different shapes and textures, so some smaller haricot combined with butter beans, or even giant butter beans, is great. Sautéing half a thinly sliced fennel with the onion is a nice addition to this vegetarian version, too.

Curried root vegetable Buddha bowl

Buddha bowls, rainbow bowls, macro bowls, hippie bowls … whatever you want to call them, they can comprise pretty much anything – but what they must be are colourful, nourishing and easy to make. This is a great recipe for using up various root veggies you might have waiting to be eaten. I've given them an Indian-inspired makeover by roasting with spices and serving with a cooling coconut and coriander chutney.

1–1.2kg/2 lb 4 oz–2 lb 12 oz root
    vegetables, such as carrot, sweet potato,
    celeriac, parsnip, beetroot
1 tbsp garam masala
½ tsp cayenne pepper
1 tsp black mustard seeds
olive oil
2 x 250g/9 oz packs ready-cooked barley,
    freekeh, spelt, wheatberries or rice
juice of 1 lemon
50g/1¾ oz baby spinach leaves
4 tbsp bought chutney or pickle, such as
    mango, lime, aubergine or carrot
small handful of toasted flaked almonds
    or coconut
flaked sea salt and freshly ground
    black pepper

For the chutney
100g/3½ oz fresh coconut
½ tsp cumin seeds
4 tbsp Greek yoghurt
small bunch of fresh coriander
1 green chilli, deseeded and roughly
    chopped
1 clove garlic, peeled and roughly chopped
juice of ½ lime

Time taken 1 hour 15 minutes
Serves 4

Preheat the oven to 200°C/400°F/gas 6.

Peel and cut the root vegetables into similar bite-sized pieces. Put into a large roasting tray and add the garam masala, cayenne pepper, mustard seeds and 1 teaspoon salt. Drizzle generously with olive oil and toss everything together. Roast for about 45 minutes, turning occasionally, until the vegetables are tender and lightly golden.

Meanwhile, to make the chutney put the coconut into a food processor and blitz until finely chopped. Heat a frying pan over a medium heat and toast the coconut and cumin seeds for 4–5 minutes, until lightly golden. Leave to cool before returning to the food processor and blending with the remaining chutney ingredients. Season to taste.

Heat the grains or rice, whichever you are using, according to the packet instructions, and season with salt, pepper and half of the lemon juice.

Roughly shred the spinach and season with salt, pepper, 1 tablespoon of olive oil and the remaining lemon juice.

Divide the grains or rice between four bowls. Top with the roasted veg, shredded spinach, coconut and coriander chutney, and bought chutney or pickle, and finish with a scattering of almonds, coconut or onions.

Flexible
Tossing some raw prawns into the roast veg is the natural choice for making this into a seafood Buddha bowl. Add 200g / 7 oz raw peeled prawns to the roasting tray for the last 10 minutes of the cooking time. Or, some smoked mackerel flaked into the finished bowls would be amazing. You'll perhaps want to cut the vegetable content down slightly, unless of course you are particularly hungry!

Massaman curry

with potato, aubergine and peanut

This Thai massaman curry is rich, spicy and full of flavour. It's traditionally made using chicken, beef or lamb with potato and peanuts, but here I have used aubergine, which has a great texture. Bought pastes are the quick, convenient option; however, if you fancy making your own, it's well worth it. The flavour is fresher, finer and more aromatic. Once made, it will last in the fridge for a couple of weeks.

500g/1 lb 2 oz new potatoes

2 tbsp vegetable oil

4 tbsp massaman curry paste – shop-bought, or see recipe

400ml/14 oz tinned coconut milk

2 bay leaves

1 large aubergine, cut into bitesize chunks

6 shallots, peeled and cut into quarters lengthways

225g/8 oz tinned bamboo shoots, drained

100g/3½ oz roasted unsalted peanuts

1 tbsp fish sauce

1 tsp palm sugar or soft brown sugar

1 tsp tamarind paste

small handful of Thai basil or standard basil

To serve

handful of roasted unsalted peanuts, chopped

Thai basil or standard basil leaves

lime wedges

Thai fragrant/jasmine rice, or rice noodles

Time taken 45 minutes, plus 1 hour soaking, an additional 15 minutes if making the paste
Serves 4

Cut the potatoes in half, or quarters if large. Put them in a pan of boiling water for about 5 minutes, until they are partially cooked though. Drain and set aside.

Heat the oil in a wok or large saucepan over a medium heat. Add the massaman paste, 2 tablespoons of coconut milk and the bay leaves. Fry for 3 minutes to release the flavour from the spices.

Add the aubergine and shallot, stirring to coat them in the paste, cooking for about 3 minutes.

Stir in the remaining coconut milk, parboiled potatoes, bamboo shoots, peanuts, fish sauce, palm sugar and tamarind. Bring to a simmer, cover with a lid or baking sheet if you don't have a lid for the wok, and leave to cook for about 20 minutes. Stir through the basil and check for seasoning, adding extra fish sauce or a pinch of salt if needed.

Serve with the chopped peanuts scattered over the top, a few basil leaves, lime wedges and rice or noodles.

Massaman paste (optional)
If you fancy making your own massaman paste, here's what you do … Roughly chop *7 long red chillies* and soak in 5 tablespoons of hot water for 1 hour. Heat a frying pan and add *½ teaspoon of white peppercorns*, *½ teaspoon of cumin seeds*, *1 teaspoon of coriander seeds* and *1 stick of cinnamon*. Roast gently until they release a spicy aroma and begin to darken. Tip into a spice grinder, liquidiser or pestle and mortar and grind to a fine powder. Add the chillies and the water, *150g/5½ oz chopped shallots*, *6 garlic cloves*, *1 tablespoon of chopped ginger*, *1 teaspoon of mild curry powder*, *½ teaspoon of turmeric* and *½ teaspoon of shrimp paste* or *3 tinned anchovies*. Either blend or pound really well to give you a smooth paste.

This will give you about 10 tablespoons of paste – plenty for two of the above curries. Any leftovers can be kept in the fridge for a few weeks, and also used as a marinade for fish, shellfish or tofu.

Mackerel, mushroom and miso broth

*This Japanese-style broth is really
healthy and packed with aromatic
flavour. I like to serve this for lunch or
dinner, but have also served up smaller
portions as a starter, which always
goes down well. Once the miso broth
is made, don't feel you have to stick
to the ingredients list. Switch things
around and use different veggies or
fish depending on what you can get …
or what you fancy.*

20g/¾ oz dried shiitake mushrooms
6 tbsp white miso paste
2 cloves garlic, peeled and crushed
1 tsp grated ginger
1 red chilli, deseeded and chopped
4 small or 2 larger mackerel fillets,
    pin-boned
2 tbsp sunflower oil
150g/5½ oz mixed fresh exotic
    mushrooms such as enoki, oyster,
    shemeji and shiitake
4 spring onions, finely sliced
150g/5½ oz silken tofu, drained and
    diced into small cubes
juice of 1 lime
flaked sea salt

Time taken 35 minutes
Serves 4

Pour 1.4 litres/2½ pints/6 cups boiling water over the top of
the dried shiitake mushrooms in a large saucepan. Leave for
10 minutes.

Put the saucepan over a medium–high heat and bring to the boil.
Add the miso paste the pan and stir until dissolved. Stir in the
garlic, ginger and chilli. Reduce the heat and leave to gently simmer
for 5 minutes.

Meanwhile, cut the mackerel into halves or quarters, giving you
smaller fillets. Rub a little oil over the fillets and season with salt.

Heat a large frying pan over a medium heat and add the oil.
When hot, add the fresh mushrooms. Toss for 3–4 minutes,
until they are turning golden. Remove from the pan, and divide
between four bowls.

Return the frying pan to a high heat and add the mackerel to the
frying pan, skin-side down. As the pieces start to curl up, apply a
little pressure with a fish slice or palette knife so the skin stays in
contact with the heat. Cook for 1–2 minutes, until the skin is golden
and crisp and the flesh is just cooked through.

Add the spring onions, tofu and lime juice to the pan of simmering
broth. Continue to keep on the heat for a further 1 minute before
ladling over the bowls of mushrooms.

Finish by placing the cooked mackerel skin-side up on top of the
mushrooms, and serve hot.

Flexible
*Instead of using mackerel, why not give some red
mullet a go? It looks wonderful and tastes great
with the broth. You can also stir in some raw peeled
prawns, allowing them to cook in the broth when you
add the spring onions.*

South Indian fish curry

with tamarind and coconut

*For this fragrant and mild curry
you make the sauce ahead of time,
adding the fish and finishing touches
when you are ready to eat it. It's best
to use fish with a meatier texture that
doesn't flake too easily when cooked,
such as snapper, sea bass or halibut.
Here I've used cod cheeks, which are
really economical. Monkfish would be
fantastic, but can be quite pricey!
I've even been known to throw some
frozen prawns, scallops and squid
into the sauce.*

2 tbsp coconut or sunflower oil

1 tbsp coriander seeds

1 tbsp mustard seeds

1 tsp fenugreek seeds

10–12 curry leaves (fresh or dried)

1 onion, peeled and sliced

1 fennel bulb, sliced

4 cloves garlic, peeled and crushed

1 tbsp roughly chopped or grated
   fresh ginger

1 long red chilli, deseeded and
   finely chopped

1 tbsp palm sugar or soft light
   brown sugar

2 tbsp tamarind paste

400g/14 oz tin chopped tomatoes

400ml/14 oz tin coconut milk

1 tbsp fish sauce

200g/7 oz green beans, halved

750g/1 lb 2 oz firm white fish, skinned
   and cut into chunks

small bunch of coriander,
   roughly chopped

handful of toasted coconut flakes

flaked sea salt

basmati rice, to serve

Time taken 1 hour
Serves 6

Heat the oil in a large saucepan and add the coriander seeds,
mustard seeds, fenugreek seeds and curry leaves. Cook for about
30 seconds, until you start to hear them crackle. Add the onion and
fennel and fry gently for about 10 minutes, until they are completely
softened and just starting to become golden.

Stir in the garlic, ginger, chilli and sugar. Stir around in the pan
for a minute or so before adding the tamarind paste, tomatoes,
coconut milk and fish sauce. Bring to a simmer and cook for about
15 minutes, until the sauce starts to thicken.

Stir the green beans into the sauce and cook for a further
10 minutes, until the beans are cooked through.

Season the fish with salt. Add to the sauce and gently stir in.
Return to a simmer and cook for 5 minutes or so, until the fish is
just cooked through, taking care not to over-stir the curry, as the
fish may start to flake.

Taste the curry for seasoning, adding a splash of extra fish sauce
or salt if necessary. Spoon the curry into bowls. Scatter over the
toasted coconut and coriander, and serve with the rice.

Flexible

*If you want to make this into a vegetarian curry, it works really
well if you add a peeled and diced large butternut squash to the
curry sauce when adding the green beans. Leave to cook until the
squash is tender. For some added protein you could then pan-fry
200–300g/7–10½ oz diced paneer cheese or firm tofu and add it
to the sauce for the last 5 minutes.*

Asian green broth

I'd eat a bowl of this every day if I had half a chance! It gives a wonderful cleansing feeling when you eat it, making you want to go back for more. I'll often prepare a big batch of the broth with just the stock and aromatics, then chill it in the fridge. Over the next few days, whenever I fancy a bowlful, it's ready to heat up and finish off by adding the fresh veggies, and that way I know I've maintained the nutritional properties and vibrant colour of the greens.

---

2 tbsp sunflower oil

2 banana (large) shallots, peeled
   and sliced into rings

2 cloves garlic, peeled and crushed
   or grated

1 tbsp grated ginger

1 lemongrass stalk, finely chopped

1 green chilli, deseeded and
   finely chopped

1 litre/1¾ pints/4 cups vegetable stock

250g/9 oz green vegetables, such as
   broccoli, green beans, sugarsnap peas
   and mange tout (use a combination or
   just one), cut into 1–2cm/½–¾ in pieces

100g/3½ oz frozen soy beans, defrosted

100g/3½ oz choi sum, tat soi, bok choi
   or spinach, stalks and leaves
   finely shredded

juice of 1 lime

handful of Thai or standard basil leaves

flaked sea salt

Time taken 25 minutes

Serves 4

Heat the oil in a large saucepan. Add the shallot, garlic, ginger, lemongrass and chilli, and gently cook until the shallots have softened but not coloured.

Add the stock and bring to the boil. Stir in the cut-up green vegetables, return to a simmer and cook for 3 minutes.

Add the soy beans and shredded stalks and leaves and cook for a further 3 minutes. Season with salt and stir in the lime juice and herbs. Serve hot.

Flexible

To make this into more of a substantial main course, you could spoon the steaming hot broth and vegetables over a bowl of cooked rice noodles. Or, for a seafood twist, add some raw peeled prawns or sliced squid to the broth when adding the green veg. Alternatively, stir through cooked prawns, crayfish or white crab meat when adding the soy beans.

mains and
sharing

Smoked haddock mac 'n' cheese

This has to be one of the best comfort foods imaginable. Classic mac 'n' cheese is hard to beat, but with the addition of rich, smoky haddock flaked through the sauce it's off the scale! Serve with a buttered green veg or My Favourite Tomato Salad (page 149).

250g/9 oz dried macaroni pasta
350g/12 oz smoked haddock, skinned
1 onion, peeled and chopped
1 bay leaf
500ml/18 fl oz/2 cups milk
50g/1¾ oz butter
25g/1 oz plain flour
150g/5½ oz grated Emmental cheese
1 tsp English mustard
2 tbsp chopped chives
freshly ground black pepper

Time taken 1 hour
Serves 4

Preheat the oven to 200°C/400°F/gas 6.

Cook the macaroni in boiling salted water for 10 minutes, and drain. Toss in a little oil to prevent the pasta from sticking together.

Put the smoked haddock in a saucepan and add the onion, bay leaf, milk and a good twist of black pepper. Put over a medium heat, bring to a simmer and cook for 10 minutes. Remove from the heat, lift the haddock out of the milk, and break into chunky flakes, retaining the milk.

In a separate large pan, melt the butter. When it's bubbling, stir in the flour. Stir for about 30 seconds, then pour in the oniony milk from cooking the smoked haddock. Using a balloon whisk, mix together until it comes to the boil and you have a loose sauce consistency. Stir in half of the cheese, and stir well until it's melted.

Remove the pan from the heat and stir in the macaroni, mustard and chives. Fold through the smoked haddock and transfer to a large ovenproof dish. Scatter over the remaining cheese and bake in the oven for 20–25 minutes, until golden and bubbling.

Flexible
This can easily be transformed into a classic mac 'n' cheese, without using the smoked haddock. Sauté the onion and bay leaf in the butter until the onion is soft. Stir in the flour then add the milk, bringing the sauce to the boil. Increase the quantity of cheese to 300g / 10½ oz. I like to mix things up a bit with a selection of cheeses such as Emmental, smoked Cheddar and Monterey Jack.

Spaghetti puttanesca

with garlic and Parmesan crumbs

This is a recipe for those times when you think you've nothing in the kitchen to cook. I'm sure you'll adapt it to suit your own preferences – for example using fresh instead of tinned tomatoes, tinned sardines or tuna rather than anchovies, or by increasing the chilli. The garlic and Parmesan crumbs are not only great sprinkled over the puttanesca, but can also be used to top fish fillets before baking or simply scattered over soup.

———————————————

3 tbsp olive oil

1 onion, peeled and finely diced

1 red chilli, deseeded and finely sliced,
  or ½–1 tsp dried chilli flakes

8 anchovy fillets, finely chopped

2 x 400g/14 oz tins chopped tomatoes

1 tbsp chopped fresh chopped oregano,
  or 1 tsp dried oregano

2 large handfuls of pitted black olives
  (such as Kalamata), halved

3 tbsp capers

400–500g/1 lb 2 oz dried spaghetti

flaked sea salt and freshly ground
  black pepper

For the garlic and Parmesan crumbs

75g/2¾ oz unsalted butter

2 cloves garlic, peeled and crushed
  or chopped

75g/2¾ oz dried breadcrumbs, such
  as panko

50g/1¾ oz grated Parmesan cheese

1 tbsp chopped parsley

Time taken 45 minutes

Serves 4

Heat the olive oil in a large frying pan over a low heat, and add the onion. Fry gently for about 5 minutes, then add the chilli. Continue to cook for a further 5 minutes, until the onion is soft and turning golden. Add the anchovies and cook for a couple of minutes more, stirring all the time, until they have virtually melted into the onions.

Stir in the chopped tomatoes, oregano, olives and capers. Bring to a simmer, season with salt and pepper, then reduce the heat. Leave the sauce to simmer for 12–15 minutes, until it has thickened.

Meanwhile, melt the butter in a frying pan and add the garlic and breadcrumbs. Toss around in the pan for a good few minutes until the crumbs are lightly golden and crisp. Tip into a bowl and immediately stir in the Parmesan and parsley.

Cook the spaghetti in boiling salted water for 10 minutes, or according to the packet instructions, until al dente. Drain well and add to the sauce, mixing well, before serving on plates. Serve with the garlic crumbs scattered over the top, offering extra on the side.

Flexible

It's the anchovies that really make this sauce something special, but if you need to leave them out, then I suggest you give some additional flavour to the sauce by adding 1 finely chopped roasted red pepper (a handy store cupboard essential) to the pan when adding the tomatoes. It's not a puttanesca sauce – but it will still taste good!

Teriyaki mackerel

with pickled veg and rice salad

This is a brilliant summery dish for sharing, whether as part of a bigger meal or served on its own. To me, it resembles a plate of deconstructed sushi, as all the flavours (and more) are represented. The rice salad is a mouthwatering combination of sweet, sour, aromatic, crunchy and soft. When eaten with the rich, spicy and salty mackerel, your senses are in for a real treat.

4–8 mackerel fillets (depending on size), pin-boned
oil, for drizzling

For the marinade
3 tbsp soy sauce
1 tbsp runny honey
2 tbsp sake or dry sherry
1 tsp chilli flakes
1 clove garlic, peeled and crushed

For the salad
100ml/3½ fl oz/scant ½ cup rice wine vinegar
50g/1¾ oz caster sugar
1 tsp black peppercorns
1 star anise
½ tsp coriander seeds
1 red chilli, deseeded and finely sliced
2 medium carrots, thinly sliced into rounds
125g/4½ oz radishes, finely sliced
½ cucumber peeled, deseeded and thinly sliced
1 banana (large) shallot or 2 small ones, peeled and thinly sliced
300g/10½ oz Thai jasmine rice
1 tsp toasted sesame seeds (see page 161)
flaked sea salt

Time taken 45 minutes, plus a few hours/overnight for pickling
Serves 4

To make the salad, heat the vinegar, sugar, peppercorns, star anise, coriander seeds and red chilli in a small saucepan until the sugar has dissolved. Remove from the heat and leave to cool.

Put the carrot, radish, cucumber and shallot in a bowl and pour over the cooled vinegar mixture. Leave in the fridge to pickle for a few hours or overnight.

Mix all of the marinade ingredients together and pour over the fish. Set aside for about 30 minutes.

Put the rice in a sieve and rinse under cold running water for about 30 seconds. Transfer the rice to a saucepan and add 750ml/1½ pints/3 cups of water. Add a pinch of salt and put over a high heat. When the water reaches a rolling boil, cover the pan with a lid, turn the heat to low and cook for 10 minutes without lifting the lid. Turn off the heat but keep on the lid and allow the rice to continue cooking in the steam in the pan for a further 5 minutes or so.

Heat the grill to high.

Put the marinated mackerel on a baking tray lined with foil drizzled with a little oil, skin-side up, and grill for 5 minutes. Baste a couple of times with the excess marinade until the fish is golden on top.

Run a fork through the rice and tip into the bowl with the pickled vegetables, removing the star anise. Mix together and transfer to a mixing bowl or platter to share. Scatter with sesame seeds and serve with the teriyaki mackerel.

Flexible
The salad is not only lovely with the mackerel, but you could also slice a couple of aubergines lengthways (about 2cm/½ inch thick). Brush with the marinade, then lightly brush both sides with some sunflower oil. Put under a hot grill for a few minutes on each side until softened and golden.

Five-spice tea-smoked salmon

This might not be the sort of recipe you turn to every day, but it's a really interesting one to do – and, believe it or not, smoking your own fish at home is far easier than you might think. I've chosen to smoke salmon fillets here, but you could quite easily do one whole piece of salmon or even trout. You'd just need to increase the smoking time by 5 minutes or so. Once you have a go at this you'll be hooked and can start trying different smoking flavours such as Indian or Middle Eastern spices in with the tea leaves and sugar.

———————————————

4 thick salmon fillets, skin on

For the marinade
4 cloves garlic, peeled and grated
 or crushed
1 tbsp grated ginger
2 tsp Chinese five-spice
4 tbsp sunflower oil
4 tbsp soy sauce
3 tbsp brown sugar
grated zest of 1 orange and juice
 of ½ orange

For the smoking mix
125g/4 oz dry rice
50g/1¾ oz black tea leaves
50g/1¾ oz brown sugar
1 tsp Chinese five-spice
2 star anise, lightly crushed

Time taken 25 minutes
Serves 4

Mix all of the marinade ingredients together. Place the salmon in a shallow dish and pour over the marinade. Cover with clingfilm and leave in the fridge to infuse over night.

Mix together the rice, tea leaves, sugar, Chinese five-spice and star anise. Line the base of a wok with a double layer of tin foil and place the smoking mixture on top. Sit a round wire steaming rack in the wok, making sure it isn't touching the smoking mixture.

Remove the salmon from the marinade and put it on the steaming rack. Cover the wok with a piece of foil and then a lid. If you don't have a lid that fits, cover with a large baking sheet. Place the wok over a high heat for 1 minute, then reduce to medium heat and smoke the salmon for 10 minutes. Remove from the heat but leave the salmon to continue smoking for a further 5 minutes.

Serve hot, at room temperature or chill in the fridge and serve cold.

Flexible
You can have real fun experimenting with different fish with the marinade and smoking mixture. I really like to use trout fillets (the smoking time needs to be cut down by a few minutes for thin fillets) and also whole portobello mushrooms or sliced aubergine, which absorb the aromatic smokey flavour brilliantly.

Stir-fried squid

with chilli, garlic and greens

If you think squid is rubbery and chewy, you've been eating it overcooked. Cooked correctly, squid should be soft and melt in your mouth. Cooking it long and slow in a stew is one way, and quick and fast is another – which is why it is such a great ingredient to use in stir-fries. Squid can be bought ready prepared, or see page 171 for how to prepare squid yourself. It doesn't matter whether you use small squid or large for this recipe – and if you have the tentacles, use those too.

200–300g/7–10½ oz cleaned squid

2 tbsp sunflower or groundnut oil

1 tbsp sesame oil

100g/3½ oz Asian mushrooms such as oyster or shiitake, torn into bite-sized pieces

4 spring onions, thinly sliced

1 red chilli, deseeded and thinly sliced

2 cloves garlic, peeled and chopped

1 tsp grated ginger

300g/10½ oz mixed Asian greens, such as pak choi, choi sum or tat soi

juice of ½ lemon

2 tbsp soy sauce

toasted sesame seeds (see page 161)

flaked sea salt

cooked rice or noodles, to serve

Time taken 20 minutes

Serves 2

Wash and pat dry the squid. Slice the tubes horizontally into rings, or slice in half lengthways and lightly score the inside in a crisscross pattern before cutting into bite-sized pieces. If using smaller/baby squid, you may also have the tentacles, which can be left whole or cut in half.

Heat 1 tablespoon of the sunflower or groundnut oil and the sesame oil in a large wok over a high heat until almost smoking. Add the squid, mushrooms, spring onions, chilli, garlic, ginger and a pinch of salt. Cook for 2–3 minutes, tossing the mixture throughout so it cooks and colours quickly and evenly.

Tip into a bowl and return the pan to the heat. Add the remaining 1 tablespoon sunflower oil and, as soon as it's hot, throw in the greens. Toss around in the wok for about 1 minute, then add the lemon juice and soy sauce. Continue to fry for a further 30 seconds or so, until the greens are just becoming tender.

Return the cooked squid and any juices to the wok. Toss around to heat through then serve on plates or in bowls with cooked noodles. Finish by scattering over the toasted sesame seeds.

Flexible

Both prawns and scallops are good alternatives to the squid, or why not try a combination of all three for a super-seafood stir-fry? For those fish-free days, sliced firm tofu works wonders cooked in exactly the same way as the squid.

Whole roast trout

with soy, carrot, spring onion and sesame

My husband Phil has recently taken to fly-fishing and, as luck would have it, has become pretty good at it. Fresh rainbow trout has been making a regular appearance on the menu at home, and we are always trying out different recipes and ways of serving it. One of our favourites is to bake it whole with a selection of Chinese flavours that infuse the delicate trout while it's baking. The end result is juicy fish, plenty of sauce and tender cooked vegetables. All you need to do is cook some rice or noodles, and you've one tasty meal.

———————————————————

approx.1.5kg/3 lb 5 oz whole trout, gutted

25g/1 oz piece ginger, cut into matchsticks

2 garlic cloves, peeled and finely sliced

2 tbsp soy sauce

2 tbsp mirin

1 tbsp honey

1 tbsp Chinese five-spice

3 spring onions, finely sliced at an angle

½ large or 1 small red pepper, deseeded and finely sliced

2 carrots, cut into matchsticks

1 red chilli, deseeded and finely sliced

1 tbsp sesame oil

Time taken 45 minutes, plus 30–60 minutes marinating
Serves 4

Using a sharp knife, score both sides of the trout through the skin, about 2cm/¾ inch apart.

Line a large baking tray with a larger piece of greaseproof paper or aluminium foil so it comes up the sides, and place the trout on top.

Mix together the ginger, garlic, soy sauce, mirin, honey and Chinese five-spice. Spoon this over the trout and, using your fingers, rub the marinade into both sides of the scored flesh, placing pieces of garlic and ginger into the slits as well.

Leave the trout to marinate for 30 minutes to 1 hour.

Preheat the oven to 180°C/350°F/gas 4.

Scatter the spring onion, red pepper, carrot and red chilli over the top of the trout. Pour over the sesame oil and place the marinated trout into the oven. Bake for 25 minutes, until the vegetables are tender and the trout is cooked through.

Serve whole at the table, flaking the fish straight from the bone.

Flexible
Whole sea bass or bream would be a good alternative to trout. If you can't get the weight I've suggested, the recipe will work just as well with 2 smaller fish. Cut the cooking time by 5 minutes. When cooked through, the flesh should just come away from the bone when lightly pressed or pushed.

Teriyaki tuna steaks

with mango and peanut salad

*Tuna has a rich, strong flavour and
high oil content, so it can hold up
to strong marinades like this one.
To balance this out, the colourful
salad is light, tangy, fruity and has a
refreshing spicy kick to it.*

For the tuna
4 tuna steaks
2 tbsp honey
2 tbsp teriyaki sauce
pinch of dried chilli flakes
sunflower oil

For the salad
1 clove garlic, peeled and crushed
   or grated
1 red chilli, deseeded and finely chopped
juice of 2 limes
3 tbsp fish sauce
2 tsp palm or light brown sugar
1 large mango, peeled and thinly sliced
½ cucumber, peeled and cut into long
   thin strips
1 shallot, peeled and thinly sliced
125g/4½ oz roasted and salted
   peanuts, chopped
small bunch of mint leaves,
   roughly chopped
small bunch of Thai basil or coriander
   leaves, roughly chopped

Time taken 30 minutes, plus up to 1 hour marinating
Serves 4

Marinate the tuna by mixing together the honey, teriyaki sauce and
chilli flakes. Add the tuna, turning to coat in the mixture, and leave
to marinate for 30 minutes to 1 hour.

To make the salad, mix together the garlic, chilli, lime juice, fish
sauce and sugar. Toss together with the mango, cucumber, shallot,
half of the peanuts and all of the herbs.

Heat a non-stick frying pan or griddle until hot. Drizzle or brush
with a little sunflower oil. Cook the tuna steaks for 1–2 minutes
on each side, basting with the marinade as they cook. Take care
not to overcook the tuna, as it will dry out pretty quickly.

Serve the sticky tuna with the salad and the remaining peanuts
scattered over the top.

Flexible
*Sliced firm tofu can be marinated and cooked
in the same way as the tuna. Other meaty fish
such as swordfish or even salmon steaks can also
be used.*

Prawn bun cha

Bun cha is a light, fragrant Vietnamese dish that consists of a sharp, sweet, salty and spicy dipping sauce, crunchy salad, rice noodles, and fried patties that are usually made from pork. Here I've made prawn ones, and they work wonderfully with the aromatic flavours – but if you want to give some tofu ones a go, check out the 'flexible' tip, as they are equally delicious.

250g/9oz raw peeled prawns
1 egg white
1 tsp grated ginger
1 clove garlic, peeled and roughly chopped
small bunch coriander, roughly chopped
grated zest of 1 lime
2 tsp fish sauce
1 tsp rice vinegar
1 bird's-eye chilli, roughly chopped
sunflower oil, for frying

For the dipping sauce
juice of 2 limes
1 bird's-eye chilli, finely chopped
3 tbsp fish sauce
2 tbsp rice vinegar
1 tbsp palm or light brown sugar

For the salad
300g/10½ oz vermicelli rice noodles
1 tbsp sunflower oil
1 courgette
1 large carrot
½–1 mooli
2 baby gem lettuce
75g/2¾ oz beansprouts
large handful each of coriander, mint and
   Thai (or standard) basil

Time taken 40 minutes
Serves 4

Put the prawns, egg white, ginger, garlic, coriander, lime zest, fish sauce, rice wine vinegar and chilli in a food processor and blend until you have a paste. With wet hands, shape into tablespoon-sized flat patties. Place them on a plate and chill for 10 minutes.

To make the dipping sauce, mix everything together until the sugar has dissolved. Have a taste and add extra fish sauce or lime if needed. You want a nice sharp, sweet and slightly salty flavour.

Cook the noodles by putting them in a large bowl. Pour over boiling water and leave for 3 minutes (or according to the packet instructions). Drain and toss in sunflower oil to prevent them from sticking.

Thinly shred the courgette, carrot and mooli using a mandolin, spiraliser or knife. Break the lettuce into individual leaves.

Heat 2 tablespoons of oil in a frying fan over a medium–high heat, and fry the patties for 3–4 minutes on each side, until golden and the prawns are cooked through.

Serve all elements separately for people to help themselves to, or place some salad leaves in the bottom of the bowls. Divide the noodles, salad, beansprouts and herbs between them, and spoon over some dipping sauce. Place the patties on top and serve with extra sauce for dipping.

Flexible
Tofu makes a fantastic alternative to using prawns in the patties. Buy 250g / 9 oz of the firm variety that holds its shape, drain off any packaging liquid and blend with the remaining patty ingredients.

Speedy prawn paella

This is a cheat's paella, but the flavour is certainly very good, and the fact that it's ready in no time at all means you really should give this recipe a go. I'll often make this with rice left over from the day before; however, the bought pouches of pre-cooked rice are ideal for this, as they tend to be sold in 250g/9 oz packs. If you keep some in your store cupboard, and have prawns and peas in your freezer, you're pretty much set up and ready to make this any day of the week.

----

2 tbsp olive oil

1 onion, peeled and finely chopped

2 cloves garlic, peeled and crushed
  or grated

2 tsp sweet smoked paprika

pinch of saffron

225g/8 oz raw prawns, peeled

500g/1 lb 2 oz cooked long-grain rice

150g/5½ oz frozen peas, defrosted

1 roasted red pepper, deseeded and sliced

175ml/6 fl oz/¾ cup white wine or
  fish stock

small handful of chopped flat-leaf parsley

flaked sea salt and freshly ground
  black pepper

lemon wedges, to serve

Time taken 25 minutes

Serves 4

Heat the oil in a large frying pan over a low–medium heat, and add the onion. Gently cook for about 5 minutes, until it's softened. Add the garlic, paprika and saffron. Cook for a couple of minutes, until the onion is rich red in colour.

Add the prawns to the pan and cook for a minute or so until they turn pink. Stir in the rice, peas, red pepper and wine or stock. Cook for 5 minutes, stirring occasionally, and season with salt and freshly ground black pepper. Once the liquid has almost been absorbed, leave to cook for a further 2 minutes to get a slightly crusty base to the paella.

Scatter over the parsley and serve with lemon wedges.

Flexible

Sliced fennel and diced aubergine are both fantastic alternatives to prawns. Add 1 small sliced fennel when cooking the onion, and the aubergine when you add the garlic. Cook the remaining recipe as above, using vegetable stock if you prefer a vegetarian paella.

Vietnamese BBQ salmon

If you've a crowd to cook for, then a recipe with minimal preparation and maximum flavour is always a bonus. Wrapping whole salmon and loads of aromatics in newspaper then putting it on the barbecue is such a great way to cook it, resulting in juicy, aromatic fish, which is also guaranteed to impress your guests.

2kg/4 lb 7 oz whole salmon, scaled
   and gutted
sunflower oil
3 limes, thinly sliced
100g/3½ oz piece ginger, peeled and
   thinly sliced
2 stalks lemongrass, finely sliced
2 red chillies, deseeded and sliced
4 banana (large) shallots, peeled
   and sliced
bunch of mint
bunch of coriander
bunch of Thai or standard basil
flaked sea salt
1 large newspaper and kitchen string
   for tying

Time taken 50-55 minutes
Serves 8–10

Heat the barbecue until it's lovely and hot, or around 240°C/475°F if using a thermometer.

Rub the salmon all over with the oil, including the inside. Season with salt, and stuff some lime slices, ginger, lemongrass, chillies, shallots and herbs inside the cavity.

Open out the newspaper, and place the salmon in the middle. Put the rest of the lime slices, ginger, lemongrass, chillies, shallots and herbs over the top and underneath the salmon, and then wrap the paper all around the salmon so it is completely covered. Tie securely with string.

Soak the newspaper with plenty of cold water, then lay the parcel on the barbecue. Cook for 20–25 minutes on each side. If the coals are too hot, the paper will burn, so keep an eye on it. You can always cover it in foil if necessary.

Once cooked, the salmon will stay hot for at least half an hour before you unwrap and serve it.

Unwrap the salmon and transfer to a platter or present at the table in the paper. Serve pieces of the juicy hot salmon with some cooking juices spooned over.

Tip
You can cook any large round fish in newspaper in this way. Cut down the cooking time if it is a smaller fish than the salmon. To check it is cooked through, gently push the fish away from the backbone. If it comes away easily it is done; if not, continue cooking.

Fish burgers

with corn relish and fried avocado

These are mighty impressive for burgers. Rather than blitzing fish to a paste in a food processor as many recipes do, I like to finely chop the fish, creating a chunkier texture and a juicier end result, much like a good-quality meat burger. Using two kinds of fish enriches the flavour, and the oily mackerel helps bind the burgers together.

500g/1 lb 2 oz skinless white fish fillets, such as pollock, cod or haddock
200g/7 oz mackerel fillet, skinned and pin-boned
2 garlic cloves, peeled and crushed or grated
1 tsp smoked paprika
1 tsp English mustard
1 tsp bicarbonate of soda
1 tbsp chopped flat-leaf parsley
oil
2 ripe avocados, peeled and thickly sliced
2 tbsp mayonnaise
4 burger buns, halved and lightly toasted
4 crisp lettuce leaves
1 beef tomato, sliced
flaked sea salt and freshly ground black pepper

For the relish
325g/11½ oz tinned sweetcorn, drained
2 banana (large) shallots, peeled and finely chopped
1 red chilli, deseeded and finely chopped
125g/4½ oz caster sugar
1½ tsp yellow mustard seeds
½ tsp paprika
100ml/3½ fl oz/scant ½ cup white wine vinegar

Time taken 1 hour, plus at least 1 hour chilling
Serves 4

To make the relish, put all of the ingredients in a saucepan, and bring to the boil. Cook for 20 minutes, until the relish has thickened and is syrupy. Remove from the heat and leave to cool.

For the burgers, finely chop both types of fish into very small pieces. Put them in a bowl and add the garlic, paprika, mustard, bicarbonate of soda, parsley, a good pinch of salt and freshly ground black pepper. Mix everything together really well, then shape into four burgers. Place them on a plate lined with baking parchment, cover and chill for at least 1 hour.

When you are ready to cook the burgers, heat a little oil in a large frying pan over a medium heat. Cook the burgers for 4–5 minutes on each side, until they are golden and just firm to the touch.

Remove from the heat and rest for a few minutes in a warm place. Return the pan to a medium heat and add a drop more oil. Add the avocado and fry for about 1–2 minutes on each side, until slightly golden. Remove from the heat and season with salt and pepper.

Spread the mayonnaise on each of the lightly toasted bun bases. Add a lettuce leaf and tomato slices, and top with the burger, then the avocado, and finally add a good spoon of the relish. Serve straight away.

Flexible
To make halloumi burgers, thickly slice 375g / 13 oz halloumi cheese. Mix 6 tablespoons of fine semolina with ½ teaspoon of smoked paprika in a shallow bowl. Dip the halloumi slices into 1 beaten egg, then coat in the semolina. Heat some olive oil in a frying pan over a medium heat and fry the halloumi for 2–3 minutes, until golden. Assemble as the fish burger above.

Fried sardine, caper and courgette linguine

*Quick pasta dishes are always useful
to turn to when time is against you.
This is a really healthy one, too, that
is packed with omega fatty acids from
the sardines. I'm using fresh sardine
fillets, which are a very seasonal, but
frozen are widely available – or tinned
sardines in olive oil can also be used.
Opt for the boneless sardines in olive
oil, and gently fry just to heat through.*

---

400 g/14 oz dried linguine

olive oil

1 large courgette

3 tbsp capers

8–12 sardine fillets, depending on
  their size

2 cloves garlic, peeled and crushed
  or grated

juice of ½ lemon

extra virgin olive oil

finely grated zest of 1 lemon

flaked sea salt and freshly ground
  black pepper

Time taken 35 minutes
Serves 4

Cook the linguine in boiling salted water, for 10 minutes or
according to the packet instructions, until al dente. Drain and
toss in a little oil to prevent it from sticking.

Cut the courgette into lengths, and then into thin strips.
Alternatively, use a spiraliser to give you courgetti strips.

Heat a large frying pan over a medium heat and add a couple
of tablespoons of olive oil. Dry the capers with kitchen paper
and add to the pan. Fry until they are golden and crisp.
Remove and set aside.

Season the sardine fillets and add to the pan. Increase the heat
and cook for a couple of minutes on each side until golden. Remove
from the pan.

Add a little more oil to the pan and add the courgette and garlic.
Fry until the courgette is softened and taking on a little colour.

Add the pasta to the courgette and gently toss together. Break or
flake in the sardines, and add the capers, lemon juice and a glug of
extra virgin olive oil, and season with salt and pepper. Gently mix
together, and serve with a drizzle of extra virgin olive oil and lemon
zest scattered over.

Flexible
*If you've no sardines at all, you could fry 4–6 chopped
anchovy fillets in the pan before adding the courgette
and garlic. Or for a fish-free option, throw in a large
handful of toasted pine nuts and scatter with a hard
cheese such as Parmesan or Pecorino.*

After-work spicy fish parcels

You'll often need a quick 'go to' recipe idea for those busy days when you know cooking will have to take a back seat. This one is a favourite in my household, as it is so simple and always tastes different, depending on the spice paste or fish I've used.

The best thing about this recipe is that there is no washing up to be done afterwards, which in my book makes it an all-round winner!

---

3 tbsp curry paste – your choice such as
  korma, tikka masala, rogan josh, etc.
1 tbsp sunflower oil
4 thick fish fillets, skin on or off, such
  as cod, salmon, pollock, hake, haddock
  or coley
4 handfuls of baby spinach
  (about 125g/4½ oz)
16–20 baby plum or cherry tomatoes,
  halved
½ red onion, peeled and very finely diced
juice of 1 lime
200ml/7 fl oz tinned coconut milk
handful of coriander leaves
flaked sea salt and freshly ground
  black pepper
mango chutney, to serve
cooked rice or naan bread, to serve

Time taken 25 minutes
Serves 4

Preheat the oven to 200°C/400°F/gas 6.

Mix together the curry paste and oil, then rub all over the fish fillets.

Cut four large sheets of foil or baking paper and divide the spinach between them, placing it in the centre. If you are using baking paper, it works better if you really scrunch it up beforehand, which makes it more pliable.

Place the fish on top of the spinach, and scatter over the tomatoes and onion. Drizzle over the lime juice and season with salt and pepper. Fold up the foil or paper to make a loose parcel. Pour the coconut milk between the parcels and tightly seal each one by either scrunching the foil edges together or using string to tie the baking paper into a pouch/parcel.

Place the parcels on a baking tray, and bake for 15 minutes.

Open up the parcel and either serve on the paper or carefully move the spinach and fish onto the serving plates and pour over the sauce. Scatter the coriander, and serve with a spoonful of mango chutney.

Flexible
As well as trying out various different types of fish for the parcels, you could also use raw peeled prawns or scallops lightly coated in the paste; 125g–150g / 4½–5½ oz per person is plenty. If you want a vegetarian option, diced paneer cheese or even some sliced firm tofu works really well.

Crayfish, sweetcorn and potato pie

I'm a huge fan of fish pie, and in the past I've always played around with different types of fish and herbs mixed into a creamy sauce to use as a filling. However, this idea came about after tucking in to a delicious crayfish and corn chowder in a seaside restaurant on the south coast of England. I've chosen to top the sweet, creamy filling with crisp buttery pastry to create one of the most tasty, comforting pies you could wish for.

500g/1 lb 2 oz potatoes, peeled and cut
   into chunks
50g/1¾ oz butter
bunch of spring onions,
   coarsely chopped
2 bay leaves
50g/1¾ oz plain flour, plus extra
   for dusting
450ml/16 fl oz/1¾ cups fish stock
250g/9 oz cooked crayfish tails
325g/11½ oz tinned sweetcorn, drained
1 tbsp chopped dill
1 tbsp chopped parsley
150ml/5 fl oz/⅔ cup double cream
375g/13 oz puff pastry
1 beaten egg

Time taken 1 hour 5 minutes
Serves 4–6

Preheat the oven to 220°C/425°F/gas 7.

Put the potatoes in a steamer and steam for about 12 minutes, until they are tender. Alternatively, cook the potatoes in boiling water, but make sure you drain them well.

Melt the butter in a large saucepan and, when bubbling, add the spring onion and bay leaf. Cook for about 2 minutes, until softened. Stir in the flour for about 30 seconds before gradually adding the fish stock, stirring to prevent any floury lumps forming. Bring to a simmer and cook for a few minutes, until you have a thick sauce.

Stir in the potatoes, crayfish, sweetcorn, herbs and cream. Season and bring to a simmer before spooning into a shallow pie dish.

Roll the pastry out on a lightly floured surface, so it fits your pie dish with some overhang. Brush the edges of the dish with the beaten egg and lay the pastry on top. Press the edges of the pastry with the back or handle of a fork to crimp and seal all around. Trim any overhanging pastry. Brush with beaten egg and use a sharp knife to pierce a hole in the top to allow steam to escape while cooking. You can use any leftover pastry trimmings to decorate the top of the pie, or just leave it plain.

Place the pie on a baking tray and bake for 20–25 minutes, until the top of the pie is golden and the filling is piping hot.

Flexible
Equal weight of any cooked fish or shellfish can be used instead of crayfish. If you're feeling extravagant, cooked lobster tails are pretty tasty!

Roast cauliflower

with anchovy crumbs and white bean purée

Roast cauliflower doesn't have to be served as a side dish: here, it takes centre stage when roasted with warm spices, and served with white bean and red pepper purée flavoured with harissa – and, to finish it off, some delicious crumbs scattered over.

I'm using baby cauliflowers as they hold their shape perfectly when roasting, and look lovely. You can of course use 1 large cauliflower cut into quarters if you choose.

---

3 tbsp olive oil

1 tsp ground cumin

1 tsp ground cinnamon

1 tsp ground paprika

4 baby cauliflowers – leaves removed

2 red onions, peeled and cut into wedges

1 roasted red pepper

2 x 400g/14 oz tinned cannellini
   beans, drained

1 tsp harissa paste

3 tbsp extra virgin olive oil, plus extra
   for drizzling

1 tbsp chopped flat-leaf parsley

flaked sea salt and freshly ground
   black pepper

For the anchovy crumbs

2 tbsp extra virgin olive oil

4 anchovy fillets, chopped

2 cloves garlic, crushed or chopped

75g/2¾ oz dried breadcrumbs, such
   as panko

Time taken 1 hour 20 minutes

Serves 4

Preheat the oven to 200°C/400°F/gas 6.

Mix together 2 tablespoons of the olive oil with the cumin, cinnamon and paprika, then rub all over the cauliflowers. Place them in a small roasting tray, and roast for 30 minutes.

Coat the onion wedges in the remaining 1 tablespoon of olive oil, and add them to the roasting tray. Continue to cook for a further 20 minutes, turning the onion wedges halfway through. By now the cauliflower should be tender throughout (check by inserting a skewer through the centre) and the onions golden. If the cauliflower needs a little longer, remove the onions from the tray and keep warm and return the cauliflower to the oven.

Meanwhile, to make the crumbs, heat the oil in a large frying pan over a medium–high heat. Add the anchovy and garlic and fry, stirring continuously, for about 2 minutes, until the garlic is soft and the anchovy has virtually melted into the pan. Add the breadcrumbs and cook for 4–5 minutes, until golden, tossing frequently. Remove from the heat and set aside.

To make the purée, put the red pepper, cannellini beans, harissa and extra virgin olive oil in a food processor. Add a good pinch of salt and pepper. Blend until you have a smooth purée. Transfer to a saucepan and heat gently until hot.

Serve the purée spooned on to plates. Cut the cauliflowers in half and place them on the plate with the roasted onions. Scatter with the anchovy crumbs and the parsley, and finish with a drizzle of extra virgin olive oil.

Flexible
The anchovies don't have to go into the crumbs if you prefer to make this a vegetarian dish. As an alternative, you can stir through a handful of grated hard vegetarian cheese at the end.

Leftover fishcakes

with caper and horseradish sauce

This recipe came about when I needed a quick dinner for a friend who was coming over. With no time to shop, I fortunately had some leftover roasted trout from the day before and a bowl of mashed potatoes from the kids' dinner. With a few other basics (and some smoked salmon trimmings in the freezer) I whipped up a decent supper. The sauce isn't essential, but I have to admit, I'm a sauce girl – so, rather than a dollop of bought tartare sauce on the side, this was far more tasty.

450g/1 lb cooked fish, flaked into pieces
100g/3½ oz smoked salmon, cut into
  small pieces
450g/1 lb mashed potato
6 spring onions, finely chopped
1 tbsp chopped dill, tarragon, chives
  or parsley
finely grated zest of 1 lemon
100g/3½ oz plain flour
2 eggs, lightly beaten
100g/3½ oz dried white breadcrumbs,
  ideally panko
3 tbsp sunflower oil
flaked sea salt and freshly ground
  black pepper
lemon wedges, to serve

For the sauce
4 tbsp crème fraîche
2 tbsp Greek or natural yoghurt
1 tbsp mayonnaise
1 tbsp horseradish sauce
2 tsp capers, roughly chopped

Time taken 30 minutes
Serves 4

Put the flaked fish in a mixing bowl and add the smoked salmon, mashed potato, spring onion, chopped herbs and lemon zest, and season with salt and pepper.

Mix everything together, taking care not to over-mix and break up the flaked fish.

Divide the mixture into eight, and firmly shape into patties. Dust each in flour, then dip them in the beaten egg and finish by coating each one in breadcrumbs, shaking off any excess.

Pour enough sunflower oil to cover the base of a large frying pan, and put it over a medium heat. Add the fishcakes, and cook in batches for about 3 minutes on each side, until golden and crisp.

While the fishcakes are cooking, mix together all of the sauce ingredients.

Serve the fishcakes hot with the sauce, and salad or vegetables of your choice, and a lemon wedge.

Flexible
If you've no leftover cooked fish, the same weight of tinned tuna or salmon would work wonders.

Baked sea bass

with potatoes, anchovies and lemon

The recipe for this tray-bake came from when I had nothing in the house to cook. The kids were away, so I needed a meal for two. This is what I came up with, and it's truly delicious – not to mention super-easy. You can easily increase the quantities to serve more, but do use an additional roasting tray, otherwise you'll end up steaming rather than roasting everything, and it's the lovely crispy bits that make this dish.

500g/1 lb 2oz waxy salad potatoes
   (such as Charlotte), cut into 1cm/
   ½ inch slices

1 medium–large lemon, cut into 1cm/
   ½ inch slices

1 red onion, peeled and finely sliced

4 fresh or dried bay leaves

4 anchovies in oil, roughly chopped

2 cloves garlic, roughly chopped

extra virgin olive oil

2 sea bass fillets (approx. 100–150g/
   3½–5½ oz each)

bunch of asparagus (approx. 250g/9 oz)

handful of pitted black or green olives

1 tbsp capers

flaked sea salt and freshly ground
   black pepper

Time taken 1 hour
Serves 2

Preheat the oven to 200°C/400°F/gas 6.

Put the potato and lemon slices into a roasting tray. Add the onion, bay leaves, anchovies and garlic. Squeeze the juice from the cut ends of the lemon over the top. Add a really good glug of olive oil and season with salt and pepper. Toss everything together and put into the oven. Cook for 30–35 minutes, turning everything a couple of times, until the potatoes are soft and starting to turn golden.

Rub the sea bass and asparagus in enough olive oil to coat, and season with salt and pepper. Place the fish on top of the potatoes in the roasting tray. Scatter over the olives and capers. Return the tray to the oven and cook for another 8–10 minutes, until the asparagus is almost tender and the sea bass is cooked through.

Flexible
Other fish fillets can be used – however, if they are particularly thick, increase the cooking time by a few minutes so they cook through. I really like using bream or mackerel, though if I'm not going to use fish at all, then 250g/9 oz halloumi cheese and a large portobello or flat mushroom make a great alternative. Prepare and cook as you would the sea bass.

Tuna poké bowl
with charred pineapple

*Poké is a classic Hawaiian dish
of cubed marinated fish, where
traditionally local fishermen would
haul in their catch and eat it on the
beach after dicing and seasoning it.
Now it has a modern approach and is
served with a base of rice, or sometimes
slaw, and topped with numerous
garnishes, pickles and fruit salsas.
Make sure you are buying super-fresh
tuna for this recipe, which is lightly
'cooked' in a delicious spicy, salty, sour
marinade. If you can't get hold of yuzu
juice, you can swap it for lime juice.*

150g/5½ oz jasmine rice

flaked sea salt

2 tbsp rice vinegar

1 tsp sesame oil

1 tbsp yuzu juice

2 tbsp soy sauce

pinch of dried chilli flakes

200g/7 oz fresh tuna, cut into small cubes

½ medium ripe pineapple, peeled and
   cut into small wedges

3 spring onions, sliced thinly

75g/2¾ oz edamame beans, defrosted
   if frozen

1 tsp toasted sesame seeds (see page 161)

½ red chilli, finely sliced

pickled ginger

Time taken 30 minutes, plus 30 minutes marinating
Serves 2

Put the rice in a saucepan with a pinch of salt and 200ml/7 fl oz/
scant 1 cup water. Bring to the boil, cover with a lid and cook on low
for 10 minutes without removing the lid. Remove the pan from the
heat, and leave the lid on for a further 5 minutes. Tip on to a tray
or plate, sprinkle with the rice vinegar, and leave to cool.

Mix together the sesame oil, yuzu juice, soy sauce and chilli flakes
in a large bowl. Add the tuna, and toss in the dressing. Leave to
marinate for about 30 minutes.

Heat a griddle and, when very hot, place the pineapple wedges on it.
Leave for about 1 minute, until you have char lines. Turn over and
cook until the other side is charred.

Spoon the rice into bowls and divide the marinated tuna between
them, pouring over any remaining marinade.

Top each bowl with the spring onion, edamame beans, toasted
sesame seeds, chilli and some pickled ginger.

Flexible
*Diced fresh salmon or mackerel are both
just as tasty as the tuna in this recipe. Fresh
cooked beetroot or silken tofu make wonderful
vegetarian options using the same marinade.*

Lebanese fish kebabs

with feta tzatziki, flatbread and charred aubergine

Absolutely any thick piece of fish works for this recipe, so it's a good opportunity to go for something you may not have tried before. Cod and salmon are both very common choices to use for kebabs, but you can mix things up a bit and try hake, coley, pouting, whiting or pollock instead.

---

approx. 700g/1 lb 9 oz thick fish
    fillets, skinned
juice of ½ lemon
1 clove garlic, peeled and crushed
    or grated
2 tsp za'atar spice mix (or ½ tsp dried
    thyme and 1 tsp ground cumin)
½ tsp paprika
1 tsp flaked sea salt
2 tbsp Greek yoghurt
1 tbsp olive oil
freshly ground black pepper

For the feta tzatziki
¼ cucumber
1 tsp flaked sea salt
1 small clove garlic, peeled and crushed
    or grated
1 tsp red wine vinegar
1 tbsp finely chopped mint
100g/3½ oz Greek yoghurt
100g/3½ oz feta cheese, finely crumbled

To serve
1 large aubergine
olive oil, for brushing
4–8 flatbreads
selection of olives and pickled chillies

Time taken 1 hour, plus 1 hour marinating
Serves 4

Cut the fish into chunky pieces and put into a bowl. Put the remaining kebab ingredients in a bowl and mix well to form a creamy marinade. Add the fish, stir to coat and leave to marinate for about 1 hour.

To make the feta tzatziki, peel the cucumber, then cut in half and scoop out the seeds with a teaspoon. Grate the cucumber flesh into a sieve and mix in the salt. Leave to drain for 10 minutes then squeeze out the excess liquid with your hands.

Put the cucumber into a bowl and mix with the remaining tzatziki ingredients. Beat together, and add any extra salt if needed.

Heat a griddle or barbecue until nice and hot. Thread the marinated fish on to skewers and place on the hot griddle or barbecue. Cook for about 6 minutes, turning a few times, until lightly golden and cooked through, taking care not to move the kebabs too much or the fish will fall off the skewers.

Meanwhile, thinly slice the aubergine and brush both sides with olive oil. When the fish kebabs are cooked, put the aubergine slices on the hot griddle or barbecue and cook for a few minutes on each side, until lightly charred and tender.

Finally, heat the flatbreads on the griddle or barbecue and serve warm along with the kebabs, charred aubergine, feta tzatziki, olives and pickled chillies, allowing everyone to assemble their own meal.

Flexible
Diced halloumi is a fantastic alternative to using fish to make the kebabs. Marinate as with the fish, and baste with the marinade while it is cooking.

Harissa and lemon-baked fish and root veg

with couscous

It's hard not to fall in love with this: big on flavour, bold in colour, easy to prepare – and, best of all, it is baked in one tray, so there's minimal clearing up! You can use any thick fish fillet you fancy here. Cod, haddock, pollock, hake, coley, pouting, whiting or salmon are just a few suggestions. Likewise, mix the veggies up if you feel like it. I love roasting radishes with the small, sweet Chantenay carrots, but you could use an equally colourful mix of beetroot and pumpkin.

---

3 tbsp olive oil

4 tbsp harissa paste

2 garlic cloves, peeled and crushed

juice of 1 lemon

4 thick fish fillets

500g/1 lb 2 oz Chantenay carrots

2 red onions, cut into wedges

200g/7 oz radishes

225g/8 oz couscous

375ml/13 fl oz/1⅔ cups very hot
   vegetable stock

40g/1½ oz toasted flaked almonds

handful of mint leaves

flaked sea salt and freshly ground
   black pepper

4 tbsp Greek yoghurt, to serve

Time taken 1 hour

Serves 4

Preheat the oven to 200°C/400°F/gas 6.

Mix together the olive oil, 2½ tablespoons of harissa paste, the garlic and half of the lemon juice. Season with salt and pepper. Use half of the mixture to coat the fish, and set aside to marinate.

Toss the carrots and onions in the remaining harissa mixture and transfer to a roasting tray. Roast for 15 minutes, stirring and turning halfway through.

Stir the radishes into the roasting tray and roast for a further 10 minutes.

Place the marinated fish fillets on top of the roast veggies and cook for 15 minutes, until they are cooked through.

Remove the roasting tray from the oven. Place the fish and roasted veg on a separate platter and keep them warm. Add the couscous to the roasting tray, stirring to coat in the harissa baking juices. Pour over the very hot stock, briefly stir, then cover with foil. Leave for 5 minutes.

Run a fork through the couscous, and lightly mix in the roasted veg and remaining lemon juice. Scatter over the almonds and mint. Serve with the fish, some extra harissa drizzled over and a spoon of Greek yoghurt each.

Flexible

Large field or portobello mushrooms are superb alternatives to fish fillets. Coat in the harissa marinade and add to the roasting tray when you stir in the radishes, giving the mushrooms 25 minutes of cooking time.

Turbot

with braised peas and lettuce

Turbot has to be one of the tastiest types of fish; however, it's also one of the more expensive, so save this recipe for a special occasion or dinner party. This is my pescatarian take on peas à la Française, which uses strips of smoked bacon cooked with the peas and lettuce. Here I've used smoked salmon, which works wonderfully well.

————————————————

3 tbsp olive oil

40g/1½ oz butter

1 large onion, peeled and finely sliced

½ tsp caster sugar

4 turbot fillets, skinned, about 175g/6 oz
  per portion

plain flour, to dust

350g/12 oz frozen peas, defrosted

250ml/9 fl oz/1 cup hot vegetable or
  fish stock

75ml/2½ fl oz/⅓ cup crème fraîche

125g/4½ oz smoked salmon, cut
  into strips

2 baby gem lettuce, finely sliced

2 tbsp finely sliced mint

flaked sea salt and freshly ground
  black pepper

Time taken 35 minutes
Serves 4

Heat 1 tablespoon of the oil in a large frying pan over a medium heat. Add half of the butter and, when it's melted, add the onion. Fry for about 8 minutes, until it has started to become golden. Sprinkle over the sugar and cook for a further couple of minutes.

While the onions are cooking, season the turbot with salt and lightly dust with flour. Heat the remaining oil in a non-stick frying pan over a medium heat, and lay in the turbot, skin-side down. Cook for 5–6 minutes, until golden brown, then add the remaining butter. Turn the fish over and remove the pan from the heat, leaving the turbot to finish cooking in the pan.

Stir the peas into the golden onions and pour in the hot stock. Bring to a simmer and cook for 2 minutes. Add the crème fraîche, smoked salmon, lettuce and mint. Season with salt and pepper, and stir until the sauce is simmering.

Spoon the braised peas on to plates and place the turbot on top.

Flexible

For a vegetarian version of this dish you could leave out the smoked salmon all together. The ideal replacement for the turbot would be a cauliflower steak. Simply cut a 1–2cm/½–¾ inch 'steak' through the thickest part of a whole cauliflower. Pan fry for 2 minutes each side in a little olive oil, then bake for 15 minutes at 180°C/350°F/gas 4 until tender.

Scallops

with Puy lentils, porcini and asparagus

This looks like a smart, restaurant-style dish. It may be impressive, but the great thing is that it's not difficult to prepare. Scallops are delicious and require very little cooking time, and are best when served a little rare in the middle. As for the orange coral attached to the scallop, it's perfectly edible. Some people like it, some don't – so you can leave it on or take if off, as you prefer. Refer to page 170 for preparation tips.

20g/¾ oz dried porcini mushrooms

300g/10½ oz Puy lentils

1 bay leaf

2 cloves garlic, peeled

3 tbsp extra virgin olive oil, plus extra
  for drizzling

200g/7 oz baby plum tomatoes, halved

2 tbsp chopped flat-leaf parsley

juice of 1 lemon

olive oil, for frying

12–16 fresh scallops

bunch of asparagus (approx. 250g/9 oz),
  halved lengthways if thick

flaked sea salt and freshly ground
  black pepper

Time taken 50 minutes, plus 30 minutes soaking
Serves 4

Place the porcini in a small bowl and pour over 300ml/½ pint/1¼ cups of boiling water. Set aside for about 30 minutes.

Meanwhile, put the lentils, bay leaf and garlic in a saucepan and cover with cold water. Bring to the boil. Cover loosely with a lid and simmer for around 20–25 minutes, until the lentils are just tender yet still holding their shape. Top up the water if you need to during cooking, then drain, remove the garlic and bay leaf, and set aside.

Heat a frying pan and add the extra virgin olive oil. When hot, add the halved tomatoes and toss them in the pan until they take on a little colour. Add the drained lentils, the porcini and their liquor, the parsley and lemon juice, and season well with salt and pepper.

In a separate frying pan, heat a drizzle of olive oil over a high heat. Season the scallops with salt and pepper and put them in the pan, cooking over a high heat for about 2 minutes on each side, until they are nicely golden.

Remove the scallops from the pan, pour in a drizzle more oil and add the asparagus. Fry for a couple of minutes while you are plating up.

Divide the lentils between four plates. Arrange three or four scallops per person and a few asparagus spears on top. Finish with a twist of black pepper and a drizzle of extra virgin olive oil.

Flexible

As delicious as scallops are, you could swap them for some pan-fried cauliflower. For this you need to cut a small cauliflower into fairly equal-sized florets. Heat a good drizzle of olive oil in a large frying pan. Add the cauliflower and cook for 3–4 minutes until deep golden. Flip over and continue to cook, shaking the pan until the cauliflower is browned, for another 5–6 minutes. Season with salt and pepper. Serve as you would the scallops.

Crab, asparagus and lemon risotto

Having a simple risotto recipe to turn to is never a bad thing. This recipe is thanks to my husband Phil, who has perfected it over the years. It's rich and creamy and there is just enough lemon and tarragon to still allow the delicate crab flavour to dominate. This is a recipe you really must try. Serve with My Favourite Tomato Salad (page 149), and a nice chilled crisp white wine, and you've restaurant-quality food in your own home.

————————————————

40g/1½ oz butter

1 tbsp olive oil

1 banana (large) shallot or 2 standard
   shallots, peeled and finely chopped

1 stick of celery, finely chopped

150g/5½ oz asparagus

1 litre/1¾ pints/4 cups fish stock

300g/10½ oz risotto rice

100ml/3½ fl oz/scant ½ cup vermouth

150g/5½ oz white crab meat

60g/2 oz mascarpone cheese

2 tsp chopped tarragon

finely grated zest and juice of ½ lemon

flaked sea salt and freshly ground
   black pepper

extra virgin olive oil, to drizzle

Time taken 35 minutes

Serves 4

Heat half of the butter and the olive oil in a frying pan over a medium heat. Add the shallot and celery and gently sauté for 6–7 minutes, until they are tender but not coloured.

Meanwhile, bring a saucepan of salted water to the boil. Cut the asparagus into approximately 1cm/½ inch pieces, and blanch in the boiling water for 1 minute. Remove with a slotted spoon and set aside.

Put the fish stock in a saucepan and keep hot over a low heat.

Add the risotto rice to the frying pan. Stir around until it is all coated with oil. Pour in the vermouth. Allow to boil until it has almost disappeared. Add a ladleful of the fish stock and stir until it is absorbed. Continue adding the stock a ladle at a time, waiting until it is absorbed until you add the next, stirring almost continuously.

When almost all of the stock has been used and the rice is almost cooked but still retains a little bite, stir in the crab, mascarpone, tarragon, lemon juice and the remaining butter, and season with salt and pepper.

Stir for 1 minute to heat the crab through.

Remove from the heat, and cover with a lid or baking sheet for 2 minutes.

Spoon into bowls and scatter over lemon zest, add a twist of pepper and finish with a drizzle of extra virgin olive oil.

Flexible

Since the crab is only added at the end it is really easy to switch things around with this risotto. 250g/9 oz of cooked crayfish, diced lobster tails or cooked prawns are all favourites of mine which work well with the lemon, tarragon and asparagus in the risotto. For a vegetarian version, I'll stir through 200g/7 oz diced goat's cheese towards the end.

Whole baked snapper
with pineapple salsa

*Red snapper is an exotic-looking
fish, with its beautiful red body and
white firm-textured flesh, which has
a delicate sweetness to it. It's often
paired with Caribbean flavours, and
when baked whole its sweetness and
moisture are locked in.*

---

1 whole red snapper, approx. 2kg/4 lb
   7 oz, or 2 smaller ones, approx. 1 kg/2 lb
   4 oz, scaled and gutted
3 tbsp olive oil
2 tsp fresh thyme leaves or dried thyme
1 tsp ground ginger
½ tsp ground allspice
½ tsp ground cinnamon
½ tsp cayenne pepper
1 tsp flaked sea salt and freshly ground
   black pepper

For the salsa
1 tbsp olive oil
25/1 oz butter
1 red chilli, deseeded and finely chopped
bunch of spring onions, chopped
1 small pineapple, peeled and cut into
   0.5–1cm/¼–½ in dice
1 tbsp rice vinegar
large handful of chopped coriander

Time taken 25 minutes
Serves 4

Place the snapper on a baking tray. Mix together the olive oil,
thyme, ginger, allspice, cinnamon and cayenne pepper, and season
with salt and pepper. Rub all over the snapper, including inside the
cavity. If there is time, leave to marinate for about 30 minutes.

Preheat the oven to 180°C/350°F/gas 4. Bake the snapper for
25–30 minutes, basting a couple of times with any juices, until it
is firm to touch and the skin is golden.

For the salsa, heat a large frying pan over a medium heat. Add
the oil and butter and, once the butter has melted, add the chilli
and spring onion. Cook for around 1 minute, before stirring in
the pineapple and rice vinegar. Cook for a couple of minutes so the
pineapple releases some sweet juices and heats through. Stir in
the coriander, and the salsa is ready.

When the snapper is cooked, serve it with the pineapple salsa.

Flexible
*This aromatic blend of spices will work well with
most whole fish so if snapper is unavailable you
could use sea bass, bream, talapia, trout, red mullet
to name a few.*

salads
and sides

Roast squash, beetroot and chickpea salad

This has to be one of my favourite salads, whether for a barbecue side dish, an accompaniment to Sunday dinner or as a handy vegetarian lunch. You can switch the veggies around, so instead of squash or beetroot you could use pumpkin, carrot, sweet potato, celeriac or a mixture. Other beans can also be used, but I do like the nuttiness and firm texture of chickpeas. Toss a handful of baby spinach leaves or watercress through the salad if you like.

---

1 butternut squash, peeled deseeded and cut into bite-sized chunks

2 raw beetroot, cut into thick wedges

2 onions, peeled and cut into thick wedges

olive oil, for drizzling

1½ tbsp za'atar (or ½ tsp dried thyme and 1 tsp ground cumin)

½ tsp cayenne pepper

400g/14 oz tin chickpeas, drained

small handful of flat-leaf parsley, mint or coriander (or a mixture)

100–125g/3½–4½ oz feta cheese or labneh

For the dressing

2 tbsp Greek yoghurt

2 tbsp tahini

2 tbsp extra virgin olive oil

2 tbsp lemon juice

1 small clove garlic, peeled and crushed

1 tbsp runny honey

Time taken 1 hour
Serves 4–6

Preheat the oven to 200°C/400°F/gas 6.

Put the butternut squash, beetroot and onion into a roasting tray. Add a good glug of olive oil and season with salt and pepper. Scatter over the za'atar and cayenne pepper. Toss together and roast for about 45 minutes, turning the veggies a couple of times, until tender and lightly golden.

Mix together all of the dressing ingredients, along with 2 tablespoons of water, and season with salt and pepper. Set aside.

Once the vegetables are cooked, transfer to a serving bowl/plate and use straight away to serve warm, or leave to cool to room temperature. Gently mix in the chickpeas and herbs. Drizzle over some of the dressing and crumble over the feta or labneh. Serve extra dressing separately.

Flexible

To create a more substantial meal, you can nestle some thick fillets of fish such as salmon into the roasting tray. Bake for about 20 minutes, or until the fish is cooked through. Remove and keep warm while you continue to cook the veggies. Serve the baked fish either as whole fillets, or flaked into the salad before adding the dressing.

Cucumber, caper and lemon salad

This could be a combination of ingredients you might not have thought to put together, but the end result is a mouthwatering salad that can be served with almost anything. The idea came from my grandfather, who would mix together thinly sliced cucumber, onion, vinegar and sugar and eat it with almost all of the meals I remember eating with him. I've added some tangy capers and aromatic preserved lemons which really do take the cucumber salad to another level – and I'm sure my granddad would love it, too.

---

1 cucumber, very thinly sliced
½ white onion, peeled and very
   thinly sliced
1 tsp flaked sea salt
2 tbsp caster sugar
2 tbsp white wine vinegar
2 preserved lemons
2 tbsp capers in vinegar, drained

Time taken 15 minutes
Serves 4

Put the sliced cucumber and onion in a bowl. Scatter over the salt and leave for 10 minutes, to draw out the liquid.

In a separate bowl, mix together the sugar and vinegar.

Cut the preserved lemons into quarters, remove the seeds and cut into small dice.

Drain any liquid from the cucumbers and onions. Add the capers, preserved lemon pieces and sweet vinegar. Toss everything together to combine, and serve.

Flexible
Beautiful silver-skinned marinated or fresh anchovies go really well with this salad. Leave as whole fillets and lay them over the top when serving, or gently mix in. Alternatively, you could use some anchovy fillets in oil, but since they are quite salty and strong in flavour I'd suggest just two or three, finely chopped and mixed into the salad.

Raw cauliflower, apple and hazelnut salad

Cauliflower has wonderful texture and flavour when left raw, and coarsely grated. Mixing it with sweet apple and crunchy hazelnuts will give you a very enjoyable salad that can be served as a side dish to any grilled, roast or pan-fried fish or shellfish.

_____

1 red apple, peeled

squeeze of lemon juice

½ cauliflower

½ red onion, peeled and finely chopped

100g/3½ oz roasted skinned
   hazelnuts, chopped

1 tbsp chopped tarragon

2 tbsp extra virgin olive oil

1 tbsp cider vinegar

1 tbsp honey

flaked sea salt and freshly ground
   black pepper

Time taken 20 minutes

Serves 4

Coarsely grate the apple, put it into a large bowl and immediately squeeze over the lemon juice and toss around to prevent the apple from going brown.

Using the same grater, coarsely grate the cauliflower, including the stalk. Add to the bowl along with the onion, hazelnuts, tarragon, olive oil, vinegar and honey. Season well with salt and pepper and toss to thoroughly mix everything together.

Flexible
I'll often make this into more of a substantial lunch by tossing in some crumbled feta cheese, chickpeas, or even flaked tinned tuna in olive oil.

My favourite tomato salad

Sometimes simplicity is best, and this recipe is exactly that. It's quick, easy and will complement pretty much any type of recipe when served as a side dish.

Depending on what is available and the time of year, you can either stick to just one variety of tomato or use a mixture colours, shapes and sizes. Whatever it is that you use, though, it is essential that the tomatoes are juicy and ripe, otherwise it's really not worth making the salad at all.

500g/1 lb 2 oz ripe tomatoes
1 small red onion, peeled and very
   finely sliced
juice of ½–1 lemon
extra virgin olive oil
small handful of basil leaves, torn if large
flaked sea salt and freshly ground
   black pepper

Time taken 10 minutes
Serves 4

Cut the tomatoes into random slices or chunks, depending on their size. Put them into a bowl and scatter over the onion. Add the juice of half a lemon to start with. You can always add more, if the tomatoes are particularly sweet and can take more acidity.

Pour over a really good glug of olive oil, about twice the amount of the lemon juice. Season with salt and freshly ground black pepper. Gently toss everything together and have a taste, adding more lemon or oil if needed.

Scatter over the basil and serve at room temperature.

Flexible
Toss in cubes of feta cheese, a handful of black Kalamata olives and chunks of cucumber for a Greek style salad.

Orange and walnut vinaigrette

It's handy knowing a good vinaigrette recipe that will complement rather than fight with a salad and all of its components. The orange and walnut flavour of this dressing lends itself to bitter leaves such as chicory, or peppery watercress and rocket. Serve with blue cheeses, crab or lobster mixed with fresh figs or pear, and crunchy walnuts.

Time taken 10 minutes
Makes Dressing for a salad serving 8

Place all of the ingredients in a bowl, and whisk until thoroughly combined and emulsified. Season with salt and pepper to taste.

Once made, the dressing will last for a good couple of weeks if stored at room temperature, out of direct sunlight.

75ml/2½ fl oz/⅓ cup olive oil
75ml/2½ fl oz/⅓ cup walnut oil
4 tbsp white wine vinegar
finely grated zest of ½ orange, plus 2 tbsp
   orange juice
2 tbsp runny honey
1 tbsp Dijon mustard
1 small clove garlic, peeled and crushed
   or grated
flaked sea salt and freshly ground
   black pepper

Flexible
This dressing can easily be transformed into a more classic vinaigrette. To do this, swap the walnut oil for flavourless groundnut or sunflower oil, cut the vinegar down to 1 tablespoon and use lemon zest and juice instead of the orange.

Spicy peanut dressing

I warn you, this is unbelievably moreish! This versatile peanut dressing can be tossed together with crunchy veggies such as shredded cabbage, carrot, spring onion and mooli to give you an Asian-style coleslaw, spooned over cooked prawns or grilled tofu for a satay-style dressing, or if left slightly thicker, used as a dip for crudités, breadsticks and prawn crackers.

150g/5½ oz roasted, unsalted peanuts

6 tbsp sunflower oil

2 tbsp rice vinegar

2 tbsp lime juice

1 tbsp soy sauce

25g/1 oz palm or soft brown sugar

2 garlic cloves, peeled and
   roughly chopped

15g/½ oz piece ginger, peeled and
   roughly chopped

1–2 bird's-eye chillies (1 for medium
   heat, 2 for a hot spicy dressing)

Time taken 15 minutes

Makes Dressing for a salad serving 8

Put the peanuts and oil in a food processor and blend for about 1 minute, until you have a smooth paste that resembles peanut butter. Add all of the remaining ingredients, along with 6 tablespoons of water. Blend until you have a smooth dressing. If you want the dressing to be looser, blend in a little more water.

Once made, the dressing will last for up to 2 weeks in the fridge. If it thickens, bring back to room temperature or add a splash of warm water.

Flexible

In addition to serving this as a dressing or dip you can also add it to a wok of stir-fried veggies and/ or noodles. The above recipe would be enough for 4-6 people in a stir-fry.

Shredded carrot and quinoa salad

This could just as easily be served as a main meal or as a side to various fish or shellfish dishes. It can be made well ahead of time, and will satisfy both vegetarians and fish (and meat) eaters. You can also mix things up a bit by switching the carrot for courgette, or the raisins for dried cranberries or cherries.

125g/5½ oz quinoa (I like to use a mix of red and white)
375ml/13 fl oz/⅔ cup vegetable stock or water
1 tsp cumin seeds
3 medium–large carrots
40g/1½ oz sultanas or raisins
½ red onion, peeled and finely sliced
small bunch of parsley, finely chopped
½ bunch of mint leaves, finely chopped
juice of 1 lemon
100ml/3½ oz extra virgin olive oil
75g/2¾ oz pistachios, roughly chopped
flaked sea salt and freshly ground black pepper

Time taken 35 minutes
Serves 4–6

To cook the quinoa, heat a medium saucepan over a high heat. Add the quinoa and toast in the pan for about 30 seconds. Shake the pan to avoid the quinoa burning. Pour in the stock or water and allow to boil for 1 minute. Reduce the heat to low. Cover with a lid and leave to cook for 10 minutes. After this time, turn off the heat and leave for 5 minutes before taking off the lid and running a fork through the quinoa to separate the grains. Leave to cool completely.

Heat a small pan and lightly toast the cumin seeds. Remove from the pan and tip into a large mixing bowl.

Coarsely grate or cut the carrots into julienne strips. Add to the bowl with the cumin and all of the remaining ingredients, including the cooled quinoa. Season well with salt and freshly ground black pepper.

Toss together to combine, and transfer to a serving bowl.

Flexible
The flavours of this salad go really well with seafood. Try adding 200g/7 oz cooked tiger prawns. Crayfish is also delicious with this combination of flavours.

Slow-cooked fennel

*Fennel really lends itself to being
served with fish, whether it is thinly
sliced and left raw in salads, where the
aniseed flavour really comes through,
or gently baked, so that the sweetness
and mellow flavour are more apparent.
This is lovely served as a side dish
to almost any recipe, though it is
particularly good with the Baked
Sardines (page 34), Crab, Asparagus
and Lemon Risotto (page 134),
Fried Sardine, Caper and Courgette
Linguine (page 112) or just some
simply baked whole fish such as
mackerel, sea bream or trout.*

---

3 fennel bulbs
175ml/6 fl oz/¾ cup hot vegetable stock
2 tbsp extra virgin olive oil
1 tbsp honey or agave syrup
peeled strips of zest from 1 lemon
1 tsp fennel seeds
½ tsp chilli flakes
small handful of fennel or dill fronds
flaked sea salt and freshly ground
   black pepper

Time taken 40 minutes
Serves 4

Preheat the oven to 200°C/400°F/gas 6.

Remove and discard any rough outer layer from the fennel, and
trim off any fronds to use later. Cut the fennel lengthways into
1–2cm/½–¾ inch thick slices. Put in a single layer in a baking dish
or roasting tray.

Mix together the stock, olive oil and honey or agave syrup. Pour
over the fennel. Scatter over the lemon zest, fennel seeds and chilli
flakes. Season with salt and pepper and cover with aluminium foil.
Bake in the oven for 20 minutes.

Remove the foil and baste the fennel with any stock. Cook
uncovered for a further 15 minutes, until the fennel is tender
and turning golden, and the stock has virtually evaporated.

Serve hot or at room temperature, garnished with the fennel or
dill fronds.

Flexible
*I've often made this dish with the addition
of 4–6 finely chopped tinned anchovies scattered
on top. They add a delicious salty contrast to
the sweet fennel.*

Charred asparagus

with anchovy butter

When asparagus is in season it's best
to make the most of this wonderful
vegetable. I love it simply steamed and
rolled in butter and crunchy sea salt,
but here's a slightly more interesting
way of serving it. If you like the idea of
the anchovy butter but asparagus isn't
available, try serving the butter with
charred tenderstem broccoli (cooked
the same way as the asparagus), or
barbecued corn on the cob, or even
some roasted onion wedges.

400g/14 oz asparagus

olive oil, for drizzling

75g/2¾ oz unsalted butter

1 clove garlic, peeled and crushed

6 anchovy fillets in olive oil, finely
    chopped (oil reserved)

grated zest of ½ lemon

flaked sea salt and freshly ground
    black pepper

Time taken 10 minutes
Serves 4

Remove the tough woody ends of the asparagus spears by either
trimming or snapping. Drizzle the asparagus with olive oil.

Heat a large frying pan over a medium heat. Add the asparagus in
a single layer (cook in batches if it won't all fit), and cover with a lid.
If you don't have a lid that fits, use a baking sheet or plate that will
sit over the top. Leave the asparagus for 2 minutes to char and cook
in its own steam.

Turn the asparagus over, cover with the lid again and cook for a
further 2 minutes. By now the asparagus should be gently cooked
through and charred at the edges.

Melt the butter in a saucepan or frying pan over a low heat, and add
the garlic, anchovy and lemon zest. Heat through for about 1 minute
to soften the garlic, without colouring it. Add a twist of pepper, and
then add the charred asparagus. Turn to coat in the butter and,
using a pair of tongs, lift it on to a serving plate.

Either pour the remaining butter in the pan over the top, or tip this
into a small bowl for dipping. Serve straight away.

Flexible
*Instead of using anchovies in the butter, you can swap
them for 2 tablespoons of chopped fresh sage. When sautéed
in butter with the garlic and lemon zest, the aromatic
sage flavour really comes through. A handful of grated
Parmesan cheese tossed into the butter at the end is a nice
addition. Both versions of the butter are also delicious
tossed into pasta for a super-speedy meal.*

Charred tenderstem

with soy, chilli and garlic dressing

This is a full-flavoured side dish that will work well alongside any Asian main course. However, I've also been known to serve this with a classic Sunday roast without any complaints! When it's in season, asparagus would be just as delicious cooked in the same way.

400g/14 oz tenderstem broccoli, washed and trimmed

1–2 tsp sesame seeds

2 tbsp sunflower or groundnut oil, plus extra for drizzling

2 cloves garlic, crushed or chopped

1 red chilli, deseeded and finely chopped

juice of ½ lemon

2 tbsp dark soy sauce

1 tbsp runny honey

flaked sea salt

Time taken 15 minutes
Serves 4

Bring a large saucepan of salted water to the boil and add the broccoli. Simmer for 3 minutes, then drain. If you are not planning to serve it straight away, plunge the broccoli into iced water and drain when cold.

Meanwhile, heat a small saucepan over a medium heat and add the sesame seeds. Toss in the pan until golden, then tip them into a bowl.

Return the pan to a low–medium heat and add the oil, then the garlic and chilli. Cook gently for 2 minutes until softened but not coloured. Remove from the heat and stir in the lemon juice, soy sauce and honey. Check the seasoning, and add a pinch of salt if necessary.

Place a griddle pan over a high heat (or preheat your barbecue). When hot, drizzle over a little oil to coat the broccoli, then place it on the griddle. Leave for 2–3 minutes until lightly charred. Turn over and repeat.

Arrange the charred broccoli on a serving plate, pour the dressing over the top and scatter with the toasted sesame seeds.

Flexible
Not only does this dressing work well poured over the charred tenderstem, it's also fantastic served as a sauce poured over pan-fried or grilled fish, tossed into noodles, served cold as a salad dressing for green leaves, or as a dipping sauce for tempura.

Lemon and bay potatoes

*Every time I make these potatoes
I wonder why I don't make them
more often! They are so moreish,
and ridiculously easy to make. There
is no worry about them becoming
crunchy all over as with traditional
roast potatoes, and the lemon and
bay flavour that they are cooked with
will go with most kinds of dishes and
cuisines, whether a traditional roast,
pan-fried, barbecued or roast fish,
tagines or casseroles, Mediterranean,
Middle Eastern... I think you get the
idea. Give these a go and you'll never
look back.*

1kg/2 lb 4 oz floury white potatoes such
   as Maris Piper, peeled
5–6 bay leaves
juice of 1½ lemons
75ml/2½ fl oz olive oil
200ml/7 fl oz/scant 1 cup vegetable stock
3 garlic cloves, peeled and crushed
flaked sea salt and freshly ground
   black pepper

Time taken 1 hour 10 minutes
Serves 4

Preheat the oven to 200°C/400°F/gas 6.

Cut the potatoes into chunks. Put them in a roasting tray big
enough so they fit in snugly and overlap rather than in a flat
single layer. Tuck in the bay leaves.

Mix together the lemon juice, olive oil, stock and garlic. Pour over
the potatoes and season with salt and pepper.

Put the potatoes in the oven and cook for 30–35 minutes, until they
are starting to turn golden. Using a large metal spoon, turn the
potatoes and return them to the oven for a further 25–35 minutes,
turning them again once or twice, until the potatoes are tender and
golden with crispy edges.

Flexible
*Using a half and half mix of potatoes and chunks
of peeled celeriac is a tasty variation of this recipe.
The celeriac doesn't become golden like the potatoes
but offers a wonderful distinctive flavour that will
complement any roast fish or seafood.*

fish preparation

/buying fish

/choosing fish

/types of fish

/preparing fish

Buying fish

The very thought of going out and buying fish and shellfish can put many people into a spin. All you need is a bit of knowledge and confidence to guide you along the way.

Use your fishmonger, farmers' market or supermarket fish counter. They should be clean, smell fresh and display the fish well.

Ask for advice and don't be scared, feel daunted or intimidated by the choices.

Always go for the freshest fish available to you.

Be flexible and use any alternatives or substitutions if your first choice of fish isn't available. There's always going to be something good to try.

Sustainability is something you should be aware of, as stocks of certain popular fish have been severely depleted by overfishing. Ask the fishmonger or look for logos guaranteeing that the fish is from a sustainable source.

Ask the fishmonger to prepare your fish for you, for example by scaling, gutting, filleting, pin-boning or removing skin.

Don't rule out using frozen fish. Often it's frozen on board the ships/boats within hours of being caught, so you can't get much fresher!

Take a cool bag with you when shopping to ensure your fish is kept at its freshest on your way home, then store in the fridge straight away.

Store fish in the coldest part of the fridge, which is towards the bottom, wrapped in a damp cloth. For added chill factor, cover the wrapped fish with some ice.

Cook within 24 hours of buying if you can. The exception is whole fish on the bone, which will stay fresh for a few days in the fridge.

Choosing fish

Standing at a fish counter looking at all of the different shapes, sizes, colours and varieties can be daunting. With so many different species to choose from you'll certainly never get bored, however the cardinal rules is to opt for the freshest fish that you can. If you know what to look out for, you'll end up choosing the best fish available.

Smell
Fresh fish smells of the sea, and not fishy at all. If it smells unpleasant, don't buy it.

Feel
Firm fish is fresh fish. Obviously different types of fish vary, but in general if it feels slack and flabby, it's not likely to be fresh. Whole fish should be stiff. Fillets should be firm and opaque.

Skin
Should be glistening and shiny, with a clear slime on the surface. Any colour, such as orange spots, yellow flecks or blue lines, should be bright and bold.

Eyes
They should be clear, bright and not at all cloudy or bloody.

Fins
Look for neat and tidy fins. Scraggy and broken fins show the fish has not been handled with care.

Gills
Bright red or deep pink shows freshness. Avoid dry, faded or brown gills.

Types of fish

There are hundreds of different types of fish that we can cook at home, but as a general rule they fall into two main categories: round and flat.

Round
So called for their cross-section, not their outline.

These include:
    White cod / haddock / hake / pollock / whiting / coley / pouting
    Pink salmon / sea trout / trout / rainbow trout
    Oily mackerel / sardines / herring
    Warm water bass / bream / mullet / snapper
    Meaty tuna / swordfish

Flat
These are flat in shape and spend most of their time on the sea bed.

They are all part of one large family and include:
    halibut / sole / plaice / dab / brill / turbot

Other
Monkfish (also known as stargazer or goosefish). This doesn't fall into either of the above categories, but is a fabulous deep-sea fish. It's the tail meat that's eaten, and it is very robust, remaining intact once cooked – unlike other fish.

Shellfish
Shells or no shells, unlike fish, none of these have a backbone.
    Crustaceans prawn / shrimp / crab/langoustines (Dublin Bay prawns or scampi) / crayfish / lobster
    Molluscs mussels / clams / scallops / oysters / cockles
    Cephalopods squid (calamari) / octopus / cuttlefish

Preparing fish

Scallops

/ see recipe for **Scallops with Puy Lentils, Porcini and Asparagus**, page 133 /

1. Wash the scallops to remove any sand from the shells. Hold a scallop in a tea towel in one hand, with the flat side of the shell facing upwards. Slide the blade of a sharp thin-bladed knife between the two shells.

2. Keeping the blade of the knife flat against the top shell, cut through the ligament that joins the scallop meat to the shell. Lift off the top shell.

3. Pull out the frilly 'skirt' and black stomach sac surrounding the scallop meat and pink coral.

4. Slide the knife under the scallop, keeping the blade close to the shell. Lift off the scallop and coral, and cut away any white ligament attached to the side of the scallop meat. Rinse under cold water. You can keep the coral attached or gently peel it away from the scallop.

Clams and mussels

/ see recipes for **Clams with Sherry, Garlic and Tomatoes**, page 48, **Smoky Haddock and Clam Chowder**, page 69, and **Steamed Mussels with Creamy Cider Broth**, page 62 /

1. Wash the clams or mussels in a colander under plenty of cold running water. Discard any open shells that won't close when lightly squeezed or tapped.

2. For mussels in particular, pull out any tough fibrous beards coming from the shells by giving them a downward tug.

3. For any shells with barnacles attached, knock these off with a knife, or scrub off with a brush.

Prawns

/ see recipe for **Speedy Prawn Paella**, page 104 /

1. To remove the head and shell from raw prawns, hold the body of the prawn in one hand and firmly twist off the head with the other.

2. Break open the soft shell along the underbelly and peel it away from the flesh, either leaving the tail attached or removing that as well.

3. If there is a dark visible line (intestinal tract) on the back of the prawn, this can be removed by running the tip of a small sharp knife along the top, and it should pull out in one long strip.

Squid

/ see recipe for **Stir-Fried Squid with Chilli, Garlic and Greens**, page 96 /

1. Hold the squid body in one hand and the head and tentacles in the other. Gently pull the head away, taking the innards with it.

2. Cut the tentacles from the head, just below the eyes, and then trim the long tentacles level with the rest.

3. Discard the small hard lump (beak) from the middle of the tentacles.

4. Inside the body there is a shell or 'quill', which looks like a transparent plastic feather. Pull it out and throw it away, and then remove the icy blue-white innards.

5. Pull off the two fins from either side of the body, along with any skin or membrane, and discard. Wash out the body pouch with cold water.

6. Cut into slices, or slice in half and then score the inner side of the squid with a sharp knife into a diamond pattern and cut into pieces.

Salt cod

/ see recipe for **Salt Cod Croquetas with Jalapeño and Lime Mayonnaise**, page 44 /

1. Pour a thick layer (about 1cm/½ inch) of salt into the base of a shallow dish. Put a thick piece of skin-on cod fillet on top and cover with another thick layer of salt. Cover and keep in the fridge for 24 hours.

2. Lift the rigid cod from the salt and rinse under cold water. Discard the salt.

3. Put the cod into a large bowl of cold water. Leave to soak for 1 hour. Unlike bought salt cod, which needs much longer soaking time (24–48 hours), homemade is far quicker.

4. Drain the cod and cook as required.

Note *If you don't want to cook the cod straight away, it can be rinsed from the salt, step 2, wrapped in muslin cloth and stored in the fridge for up to 7 days before soaking and cooking.*

Filleting sardines

/ see recipe for **Fried Sardine, Caper and Courgette Linguine**, page 112 /

1. Rub off any scales with your thumb and rinse the fish under cold water.

2. Cut off the head. With a sharp knife, slice along the belly all the way to the tail. Pull out the guts with your fingers and wash the fish.

3. Open up the belly and place the fish belly side down on a chopping board. Press down firmly along the backbone with the palm of your hand until the fish is flat.

4. Turn the fish over and pull away the backbone, which should peel out in one piece.

5. Leave whole (butterflied), or cut off the tail and slice both fillets apart. Any tiny bones can be left or removed with tweezers.

Scaling fish

/ see recipe for **Fried Sardine, Caper and Courgette Linguine**, page 112 /

1. Cut off the dorsal (top), pelvic (side) and anal (underneath) fins using
    scissors.

2. Put a few sheets of newspaper in the bottom of your sink. This will
    prevent the scales blocking it, and can just be lifted from the
    sink when finished.

3. Working under running cold running water, grip the fish by its tail and,
    working against the direction of the scales, scrape from the tail down
    towards the head using a fish-scaler or the blunt blade of a large knife.

Gutting a whole fish

/ see recipes for **Whole Roast Trout with Soy, Carrot, Spring Onion and
Sesame**, page 99, **Vietnamese BBQ Salmon**, page 108 and **Whole Baked
Snapper with Pineapple Salsa** page 138 /

1. Using the tip of a sharp knife, slit open the belly from the anal (underneath)
    fin up to the head.

2. Pull out and discard the guts.

3. Cut away any remaining pieces of the gut with a small knife, and wash out
    the cavity with plenty of cold water.

Filleting fish

1. Remove the head by cutting diagonally just behind the gills on both sides
    from the pelvic (side) fin in towards the top of the head. Cut underneath
    the head and then snap or pull it free. If the fish hasn't been gutted, some
    innards may come out with the head.

2. Starting from the head end, using the tip of the knife, make an incision along the skin on the back of the fish to one side of the backbone and dorsal fin. Use a sharp thin-bladed knife with some flexibility.

3. Return to the head end and gradually slice the flesh away from the bones, using clean sweeps, keeping the blade as close to the bones as you can.

4. When you reach the ribcage, if it's a large fish and the bones are thick, continue to cut close to them until the fillet comes free. If it's a smaller fish and the bones are fine, cut through them and remove the fillet. The fish can be pin-boned afterwards.

5. Turn the fish over and repeat to remove the second fillet.

Pin-boning

1. To remove any bones from fish fillets, lay the fish skin-side down. Lightly run your finger along the middle of each fillet and locate any bones.

2. Press the flesh next to the tip of the bone so the bone pokes upwards.

3. Use a pair of tweezers or fish pliers to pull the bone out, pulling towards the head end of the fillet so as not to tear the flesh.

Skinning fish

1. Place the fish fillet skin-side down on a dry board.

2. Hold a sharp thin, flexible-bladed knife in one hand and hold the tail end of the fillet with the fingers of your other hand. Make an incision at the tail end, just cutting the flesh but not through the skin.

3. Holding the knife at an angle, slice between the skin and flesh, from the tail towards the head end of the fillet, keeping the knife as flat as you can against the skin and board. As you reach the end, the fillet will be completely free of any skin.

Fish stock

Fish stock can be bought very conveniently in concentrated liquid, block or powder form, as well as fresh in tubs. However, it's not at all difficult to make your own, and it will probably taste far better. Plan on making it next time you either take a trip to the fishmonger/fish counter or know you'll have some leftover bones from preparing your own fish. Once it's made, you can use it within 3 days, or boil to reduce it by half and freeze in small containers. When you want to use the frozen stock, dissolve it in an equal quantity of boiling water.

1–1.3kg/2 lb 4 oz–3 lb white fish bones
   and trimmings
15g/½ oz butter
1 onion, peeled and chopped
1 fennel bulb, chopped
1 leek, chopped
2 sticks of celery, chopped
300ml/10 fl oz/1¼ cups white wine
1 lemon, cut into wedges
small bunch each of parsley,
   tarragon and dill

Time taken 50 minutes
Makes about 2 litres/3½ pints/8½ cups

Wash the fish bones and trimmings of any blood, and roughly chop so they fit into a large, lidded saucepan.

Place the pan over a low–medium heat and add the butter. When melted, stir in the onion, fennel, leek and celery. Gently sauté until softened but not brown.

Add the fish bones and trimmings, wine, lemon wedges and herbs. Pour over 1.7 litres/3 pints/7 cups of cold water. Bring to the boil and, after 5 minutes, remove any scum on the surface with a spoon and discard.

Reduce the heat, cover with a lid and simmer for 25 minutes, skimming every so often.

Strain the stock, first of all through a colander and then a fine sieve, discarding the fish, trimmings, herbs and vegetables. The stock is now ready either to use, or to cool and store in the fridge for up to 3 days, or to boil to reduce by half and store in its more concentrated form in small containers in the freezer, remembering to dilute it when using.

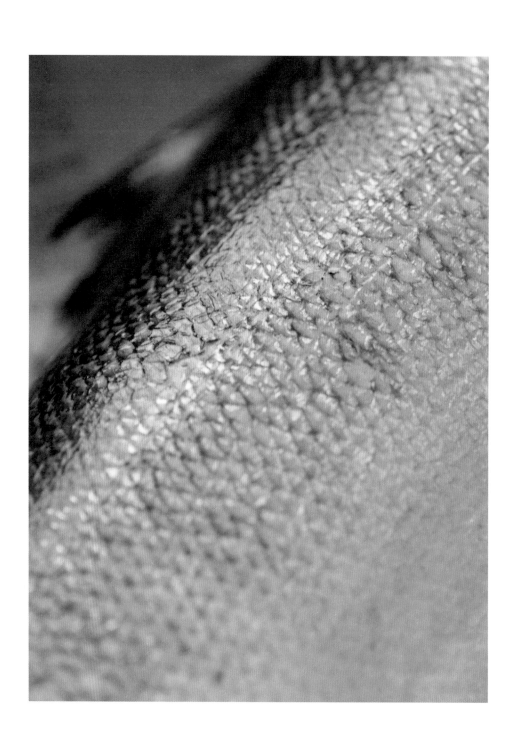

Index

Thank yous

I want to thank each and every one of you super talented, creative and patient people who have been part of the amazing team in putting this book together.

First of all, Anna Watson. Thanks for getting the ball rolling and commissioning the book in the first place. Melissa Hookway – you 'adopted' me when I was just getting started with my 'fishy adventure'. It's been an absolute pleasure working with you and your baby bump. At White Lion Publishing, I can't thank you all enough for working on the book from the design, editing, proof reading, indexing, production, publicity, sales and marketing. It never ceases to amaze me how it all pulls together.

When it came to shooting the book, we worked on some of the hottest days of the year shooting the recipes, and it wasn't easy but the iced lollies and good humour kept us going. Susan Bell, I can't thank you enough for the utterly amazing and creative photography throughout the book. I don't know how you make it all look so effortless. Alex Breeze, you treated us to awesome props that made each dish look incredible. I'm in awe of you both. Liam Desbois – fresh from uni and uber keen assistant to Susan (with your 5am starts). It was great to work with you and I'm sure you'll have a great photography career. Veronica Eijo – what a superstar. Thank you so much for assisting me on the shoot, keeping the kitchen in order and feeding us with your amazing Spanish Croquetas. I'm happy to be your taste tester anytime.

Thanks to my wonderful agents Borra, Jan and Lou at DML for your continued support and making things happen. Shame you weren't closer to the shoot and you could have tasted some of the dishes.

A very special thank you to my brilliant husband Phil, and our 'growing up too fast' children, Olly and Rosa, I know I probably turn into a monster when writing and shooting cookbooks, but I still love you. Thanks also to Mum, Dad and big sister Millie for being my sounding boards over the phone, sorry if I don't make sense half of the time.

As ever, thanks to my friends who end up being my guinea pigs even if they don't realise it. I'd like to give a special mention to my devoted pescatarian friends Claire Popplewell and Ian McGregor. You were in my mind a lot whilst creating recipes… finally one of my books that you can eat every single recipe from.

Finally (I promise)…thank you to those of you who buy and cook from this book. I hope you enjoy cooking from it as much as I enjoyed putting it together.

Happy cooking!

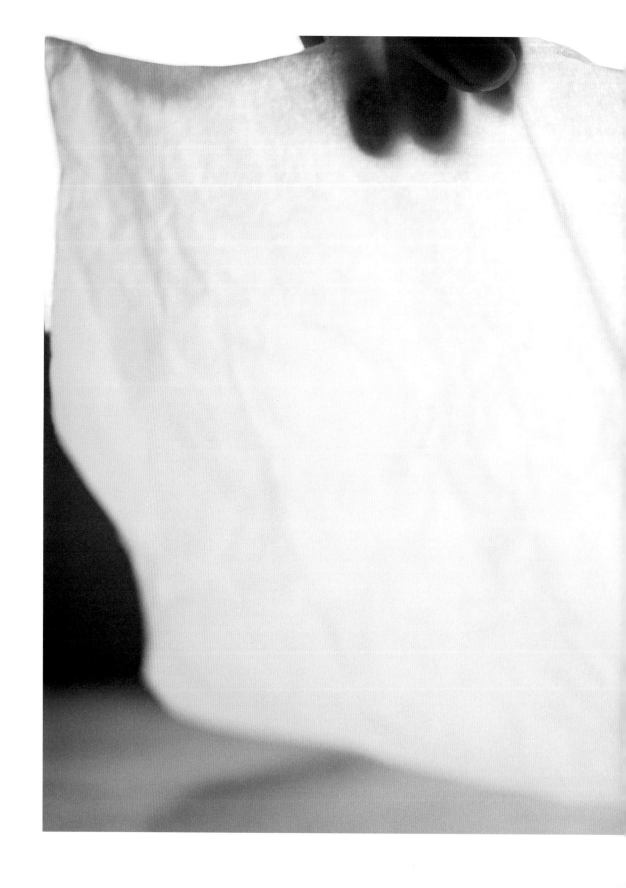